Dr. Stuart Burgess

SBSc (Eng) PhD CEng FIMechE is professor of engineering design at the University of Bristol (UK). (NB: 'Professor' is a title given only to the highest academic rank in British Commonwealth universities.)

Dr. Burgess is the designer/engineer of the NASA Space Station robotic arm and the reflector energy gathering system. His research interests include bio-inspired design, biomechanics and design in nature. He has worked in industry as a professional designer working on projects for the European Space Agency. He has published over 130 papers on the science of design and has been coeditor of the International Journal of Design & Nature. He has lectured at both Cambridge University and the University of Bristol. He is also a visiting professor at Liberty University, USA.

"This insightful book gives a fresh perspective on things we often take for granted. Jim Kraft doesn't just inspire awe in us as we read about amazing aspects of creation, he continually turns our eyes to the loving Creator. The book encourages the reader to have a deeper appreciation for both the big things and little things in creation."

Bob Devine

MBI *Nature Corner* Radio Broadcaster

Faithfully hosted the radio program for WCRF Cleveland, Ohio, for over 30 years. Produced 490 episodes of interviews about various wonders of science. Affectionately known as "Uncle Bob."

"The highest known mountain in the world is 29,035 foot Mount Everest located on the borders of Nepal and Tibet. It's the Behemoth of the Himalayas. How old might it be? Moses, that great Jewish Old Testament General writes in the 90th Psalm, verse 2, 'LORD, BEFORE the mountains were born or you brought forth the earth and the world, from everlasting to everlasting, you are God!' Think about that! Before there was anything in the skies above or oceans beneath, The Eternal God was already there. What was our Universe like *Before The Beginning*? Does that sound like a contradiction? Jim Kraft, author of this book, *Before The Beginning* asks, 'Was God bursting forth with excitement at the thought of sharing His Divine understanding and Creation to come with His future image-bearers? When love is demonstrated there needs to be an object of our love, or in this case, God's love.' John 3:16 opens with, 'For God so loved the world. . . .' 'This means you and me! God is sharing what He possesses, Eternal Life, and all that accompanies this privilege.' In *Before The Beginning*, Jim Kraft cites both an abundant amount of Scripture and Scientific examples of both truth and science all around us, showing us that wherever there is a *design*, there demands a *Designer*. What is His Name? Colossians I: 13–17 says the Designer is The Son of God, The Lord Jesus Christ. I highly recommend Jim's book, *Before The Beginning* for exciting, truthful reading."

Gerald Hillier, M.S Physics
Senior Engineer
Siemens Energy, Inc.

- 15 years engineering experience in aerospace and aviation with an emphasis on development of processes and materials benefiting the aerospace, military and energy production markets.
- Specialty: Applied Optics, Ceramics and Characterization of Materials using laser spectroscopy.

"This recent work by Jim Kraft treats the Creation of God and the relationship of God to humanity via its perception of creation, as a potential issue in a way most cannot verbalize. Jim gives a logical approach to understanding a complex issue by first acknowledging reverence to the creative genius of God with many unique, concrete examples. Second, potential motives of creation, (relative and confined to human understanding), are discussed as a means to discover God's love for humanity with the clear hope of facilitating deeper relationship with the Ultimate Designer, God of the Universe.

When applicable, examples from modern biology, astronomy, and physics are used as supportive evidence of merging creative genius and motive with God's desire for relationship; all of this is in combination with scripture relevance. However, this is not a science text, and the author does not make recurring attempts or claims to convince the reader with empirical evidence or existing counter-arguments. Rather, the reader is urged to view the creation of the universe with open eyes and open heart in an attempt to draw near to its ultimate Designer. The examples need not be put on trial as they are presented to be divinely self-evident. The tone here is not of conflict with science, but of reconciliation. For those simply looking for a re-statement or re-building of their faith, this book provides many examples, relevant, personal ideas, and relevant scriptures."

Ron DiCianni, Author and Painter

Recognized as one of the nations top illustrators. In 1989, he produced the painting that started a revolution... *Spiritual Warfare.* No stranger to the book industry, Ron has collaborated on over 50 book projects, is a six-time winner of the Gold Medallion Award for Excellence in Christian Literature and Retailers Choice Book of The Year winner with Randy Alcorn. Some of his work can be viewed at www.TapestryProductions.com.

"A group of scientists challenged God to a contest. They felt they could create a human being just as well as He could. So the contest began. God did what He does and created a perfect human being. Embarking on their attempt, they started with the same mud God did, whereupon God interrupted them and said, *"Go get your own mud . . ."* That's the story in a nutshell, isn't it? God either is or He isn't. And if He is, our attempts to erase Him, preclude Him or override Him will never work. Someday it will become much clearer than it is right now, but by then it will be too late to recant. This book may help you come to the truth of God before that day, for the truth, dear reader, is that it doesn't matter what you believe. It's only matters what is true."

Kay Kyllonen, Pharm.D., FPPAG,
Neonatal ICU Clinical Pharmacy Specialist

Clinical Pharmacist in Pediatrics, mother of two

"I am enjoying this book. I have been reading it with my Bible. I love the integration of Scripture, science (which in its truest form never contradicts the word of God) and concepts of design you use to enliven the reader's perception of God. I will be recommending it to others as an engaging look at the study of God's creation. Thanks for giving me the privilege to review your (and His) handiwork."

Michael Card
Singer-songwriter, musician, author, radio host

Song's include: *El Shaddai, Immanuel, Joy in the Journey,* and *Heal Our Land.* Michael has authored over 25 books. His new book is titled: *Inexpressible: Hesed and the Mystery of God's Lovingkindness.*

"Look as far out with the most powerful telescope and it is there, color, structure magnificence. Look as far in as you possibly can with an electron microscope and it is there, design, function, beauty. Look up or all around you, or down... you cannot escape the intricate craftsmanship of every tree, leaf, insect, bird, flower, wave, raindrop, sunset, grain of sand. We stand before it all without excuse (Rom.1: 20). Without an excuse for not wondering, not appreciating, not giving thanks. Jim's book reawakens and reminds us of all this and more. It instructs us to look in places we never thought to look. Most of all it redirects the wonder to the Creator Himself. It provides the proper Point of Focus for all our appreciation and thanksgiving."

BEFORE THE BEGINNING
...God Designed

Jim Kraft

BlossomRidge
BOOKS

Mentor, OH 44060

Blossom Ridge Books printings: January 2013, July 2019

www.blossomridgebooks.com

ISBN 13: 978-0-9884652-3-7
eBook ISBN 13: 978-0-9884652-0-6

Library of Congress Control Number: 2019944275

Cover Design: Jim Kraft

Editor: Linda Cizek
Assistant Editors: Tamara Kraft, Lynne Koles

Background Illustration: Painted by Achim Prill,
PRILL Mediendesign & Fotografie
Front Cover Photo: Jim Kraft
Back Cover Photo: The Visual MD
Back Cover Photo: Jurgen Otter

Book Production: Blossom Ridge Books

Animals, leaf, and DNA/Fish Emblem Photo Illustrations: Jim Kraft
DNA Strand Illustration: Hakusan
Giraffe Photos: Fotilia.com
Woodpecker Photo: Andrei Stroe
Incubator Bird Photo: J.J. Harrison
Owl Butterfly Photo: Didier Descouens
Monkey Face Orchid Photo: Butterfield

Blossom Ridge Books Contact Info: 1-888-572-3899.

Printed in the United States of America

Dedicated to my Mom, Mike Murray and to those who find themselves asking, *What's this all about anyway?* And to those who enjoy epiphanies!

Contents

Acknowledgments

This book would not have been possible without the faithful support of my wife Tammy. She has taken on extra jobs to help see this endeavor through to its completion. She was able to assist greatly in making my out-of-the-box ideas worth taking to heart. She made the read smoother and more concise.

A spirit-filled friend, Alan Dyczewski, offered words of wisdom to help me keep the book on track. This work is a mission from God, with His Word as the foundation of everything I wrote. Alan's sensitivity to spiritual matters was invaluable.

Long-time friends, Tony and Sue Masevice, offered much needed encouragement mid-stream. Tony's in-depth knowledge of scripture and his gift of discernment were essential in keeping the project biblically sound. Sue helped address the expectations of the reader.

I would like to thank my daughter Lynnea. As a college student, she was a sounding board for readers in that age bracket. Lynnea also helped me to express this message in a way that brought the love of God to the forefront, rather than the judgment of God.

My son Jared is a leader in the making. He enjoys nature and discovering all that he can about the amazing creatures God has made. His energy and excitement is contagious and reminds me to look at all creation with a sense of awe and wonder.

The prayer warrior on this project was Marianne Murray Dyczewski. I will always remember her faithfulness. The uncanny timing of outside influences that continually happened during the course of this project and even in the second edition would astonish anyone. This was my encouragement to keep driving forward.

The wisdom and big-picture perspectives of Wayne and Marcy Sacchini were of great help in the growth of my own spiritual sensitivity. I have learned to raise my spiritual antenna each time they hand me an article or something of interest.

Doug Rhode guided me in a few areas of research which gave the project more meaningful application. I thank Kevin O'Reilly for his kindness and wisdom.

My editor, Linda Cizek, was Godsent. She patiently looked past my rough edges and saw the vision that God had put on my heart. Her interest in the arts and natural science, her creativity and her passion for life as God intended it to be, along with her God-given talents and abilities, fully blessed this mission beyond my expectations. I do not know where the project would be without her.

Lynne Koles was very kind in making my second edition edits a smooth read. Her observations on content arrangement were very insightful as well. I am taken aback as I think about what a blessing she was.

I am thankful for long conversations with Mike Murray and, although he is now present with the Lord, he will never be forgotten. As a patent contributor on cancer research, Mike unknowingly piqued my interest in science and how our Creator God's handiwork can be seen and considered. His kindness and friendship made a deep and lasting impact on me.

I am extremely grateful for God's provision for our needs during the writing of this book. To all of those who answered God's call and provided encouragement, prayers and (sometimes even cash), I thank you. Without these committed supporters, I would have never been able to complete this work.

This book only became a reality by the generous giving of time and insight from all these individuals. My prayer is that God would continue to use these people of great influence to further kingdom building during this window of opportunity.

Preface

The reason for writing this second edition is twofold. America has lost its way. Suicides are up, depression and anxiety is skyrocketing. Psychologists are now seeing an unprecedented rise in narcissism. Something is changing the way we think and interact, causing our society to become a socially inept train wreck. It seems that more and more people are focusing on the negative and have lost their ability to see the big picture. In the late 1990's, human-to-machine-to-human communications took a leap in technology. Not addressing these issues is irresponsible.[1]

Something in our society is devaluing human life. Could our new forms of communications be desensitizing us to human interaction—to love?[2]. *Before the Beginning...God Designed* rips through the perspective-blocking lies to help us flawed humans see truth. Then, with God's help, life balance and objectivity can be restored.

The second reason is timing. Now is the time to read this book. By taking a journey to the beginning of things, you will discover a perspective-restoring remedy that God gave us through His servant Job. This meager attempt to put God back into our country can happen one heart at a time. God reveals himself to man in three ways, through His Word, through His Son, and through Creation.[3] *Before the Beginning... God Designed* helps us to consider creation foundations.

A Messenger

I am a communications designer by trade with classes in psychology and marketing. For maintaining objectivity, I have 30 years of taking and leading Bible studies in my local church. I have worked with many start-ups companies, church and parachurch ministries launching their dreams. I introduced three national brands. I have worked with large, blue-chip companies like GE, American Greetings, and Petro Canada which have entrusted me with motivational and promotional communications—the guy who can mix the research, arts, and a headline to get a message across. However, these are not the experiences that I feel qualify me to write on the subject. In fact, is their really anybody qualified enough to write about transcendent creation origins? The Word/Power of God speaks for itself and underlines the points made throughout this book. My spiritual gift is discernment. One of the aspects of this gift is the ability to ask the right questions at the right time. Many of the marketing personnel of corporations I have worked with have made comments like this one: "No one is asking the needed questions like you are, congrat's you have the project."

Twenty years of my life, I feel, have been in the middle, in between things yet to come, a place to observe, a place to feel the real pains of need and tragic loss. So much so, the desire to thrive has been threatened—where hope has been removed—a frightening place to be. Our family has experienced financial and real estate holdings loss including a farm and business loss. We've dealt with cancer, the death of loved ones—life in its difficult areas of change. These types of life events can distort or even break our perspective.

I have also lived out specific chapters in the book, where only hands-on experience can be the real instructor. I have referenced over 70 experts in unique areas in science and research as well as multiple translations of scripture.

Cross-discipline degrees are not offered by colleges to walk you through these life challenges or see life from a creator's viewpoint. I have not only been at the bottom of the barrel, but underneath the barrel with the crawly things as well. With that said, I can say with confidence, that a faith walk with a loving, Creator-God can offer a perspective of another kind.

Tim Mackie, Ph.D. of the Bible Project makes a wonderful observation about man's stewardship of creation in his Science and Faith presentation made in August of 2017.[4] He states that all humans, male and female are royal stewards of the beauty, meaning, and order of His creation. My hope is that this writing will, in some minute way, assist in this stewardship.

Introduction

If we are so blessed to be able to experience the beauty of God's creation, it is natural to begin to contemplate how and why this world came into existence. I have heard that many recent Christian converts weren't able to see beauty until after their conversion. Something happened within their spirits—a gift bestowed from above—a creation reveal of sorts. What a vast repertoire of gifts our Creator (with a capital C) encompasses! Some people have been granted the skill to paint, or to play music or to design things, but they require tools and inspiration. The new converts were given the ability to simply see things differently.

Think about it—God has the ability to create something from absolutely nothing! There were no bowls of fruit or beautiful seascapes or memorable characters in God's life to serve as His inspiration. When God Creates, He starts with nothing. $(-\infty) + (+\infty) = (\quad)$ The space between the brackets is empty on purpose. I couldn't use the number zero as "0" between the brackets because that is a number.

In that sense, we're not really Creators of anything (with a capital C)! However, I would say that we are *creators of lesser things*. We take great pride in working with all that God has given us and we try diligently to do the very best we can. He gave us thought generation and creative capabilities. But none of these great creation thoughts can compare with the ideas of God, the Alpha and Omega. We are encouraged to "consider creation" throughout the Bible.

> *I remember the days of long ago; I meditate on all your works*
> *and consider what your hands have done.*

Psalm 143: 5 (NIV)

Today, our days are overflowing with commitments and the pressures of everyday living. Unfortunately, a jam-packed and hectic life can burden our hearts and weigh us down, like an over-stuffed suitcase that we drag by our side as we trudge through a busy airport. Daily "busy business" can cause us to miss the blessings and insights that can come through by simply taking a little time to "consider these things." When we finally do, we can truly begin to see the Master's handiwork and creative genius.

There is another spirit in the air—and it's very illusive. Even within the church, something seems to have gone awry, but we're not quite sure what. Survival instincts seem to be put on the back burner. A sense of valor to protect what is good seems to be missing. Where's the outcry on societal atrocities? Where's the contrition and remorse? It appears that a spectator mentality is prevailing as our religious freedoms are being threatened.

Could it be that we are feeling the affects of a society that has removed God? Has God given us or our loved ones over to reprobate minds (a mind without moral compass or beyond hope of salvation). Or, have we unknowingly latched on to idols and have created other gods? Have we distracted ourselves to a point where we can't even see that there is a problem, a personal need for humility?

In the book of Job, Job lost his perspective. God stepped in and declared who He is. God used creation, reminding Job of creation's blueprint to adjust Job's outlook. Perhaps we have lost our perspective too.

When we consider the care and utter brilliance that went into creation—the transcendent, sacrificial love that God has for us—it cannot help but change us.

My initial hope for this book is that it will cause us to look at creation in a new light; that we might see creation as an event which points to God's complete plan for humanity. I pray that this book will be used as a tool, an actual *agent of change*, which will help you to discover the Creator's deep passion that was behind it all. That passion is an incredible gift, sent directly from the heart of God to you and me.

Please take note on how I use the word passion. On page 21 there is a somewhat poetic clarification titled: *The Angst of Passion*.

Why the name?

There are 300 scriptures that communicate that thought precedes actions.[1] John 17: 24 states: "God loved us before the foundations of the world." The book's name, *Before the Beginning...God Designed*, could have had other tags reading: *...God Loved*, *...God Authored* or *...God Engineered*. What all of these tags have in common is that they are all transcendent thought, made complete through action. Merriam-Webster defines transcendent; "exceeding usual limits." Repetition creates emphasis. The 300 scriptures mentioning thought gives heed to the importance of thought.

Dr. Caroline Leaf, Ph.D., Communication Pathology, BSc in Logopedics and Audiology defines the miracle of thought in her work thoroughly. At such a time as this, we can now see the molecular make-up of the brain. She describes the miracle of thought. The time before Genesis is when God designed the 'knitting patterns' of human development, you and me, in our mother's wombs. I am sure much consideration was given to reaching our stubborn hearts as well. God was there, thinking and planning, before the existence of *anything*:

> *Father, I desire that they also, whom You have giv-*
> *en Me, be with Me where I am, so that they may*
> *see My glory which You have given Me, for You*
> *loved Me before the foundation of the world.*

John 17: 24

> *Before the mountains were born or you brought forth the earth*
> *and world, from everlasting to everlasting you are God.*

Psalm 90: 2 (BSB)

When asked about our own ideas about how the world began, it is easy to default to a "just add water and stir" answer: God spoke and it happened. However, when we attempt to think about the planning that went on *before* God spoke the world into existence, the awesome nature of this act can fill us with wonder.

As we work toward understanding our limited creative process, we can apply what we learn to the biblical picture of God and His works. This can help us better understand His creation. We can begin to recognize the incredible, loving forethought that God put into every divine act described in Genesis. Furthermore, we discover that God is *still* passionate about us. He calls out to us in a very real and tangible way. He desires to show us He is close to us, as a father longs to be with his child. To live and die on this planet without giving credence to the God who created this universe will not only result in missed personal blessings, it will ultimately affect our eternal destiny—a tragic consequence indeed.

> *For since the creation of the world His invisible attributes, His*
> *eternal power and divine nature, have been clearly seen,*
> *being understood through what has been made, so that they*
> *are without excuse. For even though they knew God, they did*
> *not honor Him as God or give thanks, but they became futile*
> *in their speculations, and their foolish hearts were darkened.*
>
> Romans 1: 20–21

After God completed planning and designing the universe, creation commenced. By His Word, God spoke all into existence:

> *Then God said, "Let there be light," and there was light.*
>
> Genesis 1: 3

In the beginning, therefore, God was central to the abyss of the universe, less the stars, sun, moon, galaxies, and even space as we know it! The gospel of John opens with the words, "In the beginning was the Word, and the Word was with God, and the Word was God." He is eternal. God's other attributes include: omniscience, omnipresence and omnipotence! Our understanding is limited, but God has no limits. Is it possible to go beyond our current capabilities of understanding in our finite state? Can we push the limits of understanding as we investigate this topic, even when His creative power and genius are inconceivable? If we can gain a stronger sense of God's identity and learn what His *mission* is, then perhaps the worship that we express back to God may be better focused and more passionate.

God reveals Himself in creation. The 1980 volcanic eruption of Mt. St. Helen's reveals a narrative worth considering. Isaiah 2 reveals that it is in God's character to shake the earth in the day of our Lord. The Bible teaches that God is a jealous God. In Deuteronomy, Moses writes,

For the LORD your God is a consuming fire, a jealous God.

Deuteronomy 4: 24 (NKJV)

The clearest sensation that a human being has when he experiences the holy is an overpowering and overwhelming sense of creatureliness. That is, when we are in the presence of God, we are humbled and become most aware of ourselves as creatures. This is the opposite of Satan's original temptation, 'You shall be as gods.'[2]

R.C. Sproul

This profound statement stems from Psalm 19:1, "The Heavens declare the glory of God." We should be the generation that gets out of the way of God's glory.

I hope that when you are finished reading this book, you will understand that you are at the very epicenter of God's passion and that this realization will begin an ardent quest to learn more about our loving Creator. My second hope is that you will be able to look past the propaganda society is perpetuating, and simply ponder the wonder of creation in its purest sense.

Before the Beginning. . . God Designed weaves together many of life's unanswered questions regarding perplexing events. Finding a connection between the invisible, intangible spiritual realm and the visible, concrete world will help to settle and clarify many of these perplexities. My desire is to demonstrate how art, science and the natural world all work together to reflect the glory and creative genius of the Ultimate Designer—the Lord of the Universe. I pray that this will allow you to develop a deeper relationship and appreciation for our Creator and, in turn, you will be able to see the world around you with fresh new eyes and a renewed sense of peace and wonder!

You may even learn how to engage the creative and visualization process more quickly. I pray you will strive to be curious and to ask deeper questions. You might just come away from this book seeing life from a completely different point of view!

The purity, the wholeness and completeness of heart, mind, body and soul that God intended for us before the beginning is truly something to contemplate. The old can become new again when we come to know God for who He really is: the Planner, the Designer and the magnificent Creator of all things!

> He made the universe to get glory for grace. Is it the
> sweetest sound/taste of your guilt ridden soul?[3]
>
> John Piper

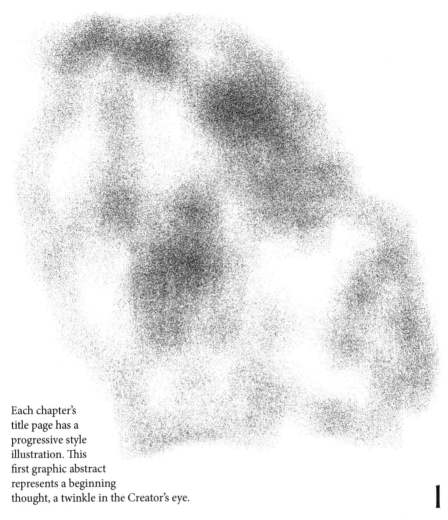

Each chapter's title page has a progressive style illustration. This first graphic abstract represents a beginning thought, a twinkle in the Creator's eye.

I

What Was He thinking?

I just broke out sobbing as I witnessed teens and some other folks, see something they've never seen before. The one teen gasps for air, he looks left then right, shaking his head in disbelief. He sobs and shouts: "Oh my God it's different, it's different"! Then an older gentleman swinging his arms, bursts out in tears, trying to hold back a childlike joy he never felt before. Another teen exclaims and sobs simultaneously, "Oh my God, is this what the real world looks like?" These color blind people are seeing color for the first time, with specially made glasses. So what's happening here—those who experience this miracle simply cry out in elation? Somehow the core of their being connected the big picture dots instantly. A knee-jerk reaction of gratefulness, expressed by tears, engages as the gift of sight is acknowledged. They're living in a significant moment—their souls somehow knew it as the spirit within them recons with truth.

What was on God's mind when He was creating the gift of sight? What prodded Him to create conscious *beings that could get this kind of message*? What was God thinking about prior to Genesis, prior to all that we see—and don't see: underwater creatures, land animals, underwater plants, plants on the earth, plants that grow in the air, man, woman, the earth, the atmosphere, the planets, gravitational pull, the stars, the sun, the galaxies. . . everything! Why does He produce such heart-touching beauty everywhere? What about the precision found in life-sustaining order? His fingerprint is on every top, bottom and middle layer of existence! His creation begs intrigue and mystery as God displays His touch on all of creation. The story of the color blind seeing for the first time tells us a few things. The first is how much we take for granted. And the second, a heart truth makes it home for the first time.

> *For by him all things were created: things in heaven and on earth, visible and invisible, whether thrones or powers or rulers or authorities; all things were created by him and for him.*
>
> Colossians 1: 16 (NIV)

The many mysteries of God are something to ponder. We get a very small grasp of the amount of 'thoughts,' which many are mysteries when we think of the verse:

> *How precious to me are your thoughts, O God! How vast is the sum of them! Were I to count them, they would outnumber the grains of sand—when I awake, I am still with you.*
>
> Psalm 139: 17–18

Why did He create us?

I can imagine a truck load of sand or a satellite view of a huge desert, but to envision an actual number of grains, not so much. However, if the Word of God says it, and it is indeed the final authority, we can bank on that information. In chapter 3, Jason Lisle, Ph.D., Astrophysicist, takes a shot at determining an actual granular count.

Charles Spurgeon, a nineteenth century preacher, commented on God's thoughts: "...the Preserver, the Redeemer, the Father, the Friend, are evermore flowing from the heart of the Lord. Thoughts of our pardon, renewal, upholding, supplying, educating, perfecting, and a thousand more kinds perpetually well up in the mind of the Most High. It should fill us with adoring wonder and reverent surprise."

God has given us gifts of creativity, the ability to wonder, and the ability to ask some very deep and intriguing questions. How much of ourselves do we invest in our quest for truth when He is orchestrating so much for us? In the book of Matthew, when asked by the Pharisees which commandment of the Law was the greatest, Jesus responds:

> *You shall love the Lord your God with all your heart*
> *and with all your soul and with all your mind.*

Matthew 22: 37

According to these words, we are to give our all, a "passionate pursuit" in getting to know the Creator, His creation and all things of God! Searching the deeper things of God (profound and bottomless) also takes a work of the Spirit of God, which may or may not *reside* in us.[1] *If* the Spirit resides in us, then understanding will come more easily.

One deep questions is "Why did He create us?" Was God bursting with excitement, wanting to share His creations to come and divine understandings with His children—us? In John 3: 16, God is described as a *compassionate* God. God is also beyond generous, sharing not only this earthly life but eternal life and all that accompanies this privilege as well. God's love is expressed by His intense passion for all of mankind by offering up His Son in a death sacrifice to restore the fellowship that He once experienced with Adam and Eve in the Garden of Eden.

What was God thinking with such a sacrificial act? The relationship is certainly one that we can identify with—a father and a son—but the sacrificing of that cherished child for the salvation of all mankind? This was an act beyond all human comprehension; a loving deed intended to save. Ultimately, this would become humanity's single most impactful act of all time.

> *Your eyes saw my unformed body. All the days ordained for me were written in your book before one of them came to be.*
>
> Psalm 139: 16 (NIV)

God was entering names in the Book of Life before He even formed the world! This verse implies that there is a dimension and a beginning where time doesn't exist. That is such an amazing thought! In order to be able to do this, He had to give names to those before and after us. He knew we would struggle to comprehend this idea upon reading it. Were these verses intentionally written for us to get a glimpse into this timeless dimension—like a child peering into a gigantic telescope with a special lens filter that can peek into another dimension?

Richard A. Swenson M.D., is a physician and a futurist with a B.S. in physics, Phi Beta Kappa from Denison University. He states, "If God operates in more than one time dimension, it means that He can move around within our single time dimension and see everything happening simultaneously." God sees, not only our dimension but all of creation, inclusive of time and space, the same way.

Our challenge is to keep an open mind as we look into a place where all is still and time has no meaning. If a clock were somehow placed in that dimension, the second hand would suddenly stop. There would be no hurry to do anything. However, a flurry of activity would surround our Creator as He designed and orchestrated all life events. He already knew that it would all be recorded in the pages of His written record, from Genesis to Revelation, as well as each name written in the Book of Life.

All of this was done with intentional and unfathomable love; Pure creation! Pure intention! Pure passion! The Bible also reveals His absolute desire for *true* friends[2]... and thus, He created man. God wants us to be living in harmony with Him—in perfect orchestration as we follow His melody to fulfill His divine plan. Like the beautiful and unique instruments of an orchestra, each one of us has a different purpose to discover and a different part to play.

> God, in His wisdom, even gave us the gift of the Bible—the unprecedented message of passion meant to save and lift the condition of our hearts.

He has given us independence and free will. Why did God desire to create such independent beings, capable of deep thinking and creative action? Perhaps He did this to confirm our individual identities. He knew it would take the sacrifice of time and energy to focus on the journey of *putting Him first*. Could this be a test of our genuineness in the pursuit of knowing our Creator?

It took divine careful thought to create us and all that we see. God, in His wisdom, gave us the gift of the Bible—the unprecedented message of passion meant to save, lift the condition of our hearts and point us to Him. If we learn to look at things of creation in a different light, we can gain insight into the heart and intent of God.

What was God thinking when He was creating? His thoughts are beyond what we are capable of grasping, He wrote his action-packed, metaphor filled "love letter" in a form that would be understandable to His people. Words are almost useless in describing God's mind and ways:

For My thoughts are not your thoughts, Nor are your ways My ways, declares the LORD. For as the heavens are higher than the earth, So are My ways higher than your ways, And My thoughts than your thoughts.

Isaiah 55: 8–9

God desires for us to utilize our finite and limited thinking to understand His infinite and unlimited ones.

Who can fully grasp the infinite capacity of God's mind?

He has also set eternity in the hearts of men; yet they cannot fathom what God has done from beginning to end.

Ecclesiastes 3: 11 (NKJV)

God created in us a desire to utilize our limited capability for thinking to understand His infinite thoughts. In his book entitled *In the beginning was information,*[3] scientist Dr. Werner Gitt, former director and professor at the German Federal Institute of Physics and Technology, explains the incredibly intricate orchestration found in nature. Dr. Gitt comments on how we take for granted the presence of information that organizes every part of the human body, from hair color to the way our organs function. He makes it clear that life has an enormous amount of organized data that is processed and synthesized by "an originator." Another doctor, Richard A. Swenson, states in his book, *More than Meets the*

> "... If we observe design, it is not wrong to infer a designer."
>
> Richard A. Swenson,
> *More Than Meets The Eye*

Eye, ". . . If we observe design, it is not wrong to infer a designer."[4] Both doctors concur. There was (and still is) a process in place, but before it was set into motion, there was motive and very clear design.

How painstakingly meticulous the Designer of the universe was in His work! God went through the trouble of personally naming all the stars and He even knows if one is missing. Moreover, the power of His omnipotence is incredible. For example, He asks us to pray to Him. There are roughly seven billion people on the planet, each with a potentially long list of prayers. Yet, we have a God who can handle the volume.

Not only are God's thoughts far beyond our understanding, but *He also has the capacity to store, process, sort, analyze, create, trouble shoot, plan and initiate series of events for the common good. He coordinates these events while simultaneously preparing hearts to learn and grow closer to Him.* He lovingly guides us through this earthly life. Amazingly, each of our human prayers intersects with His pre-determined will. He moves and inspires others through His patient teaching, and His gentle nurturing, then proceeds in His perfect timing.

The LORD works out everything to its proper end—

Proverbs 16: 4 (NKJV)

A perfect illustration of this idea was developed in the movie *Spiderman II*. To seek revenge for his father's death, Harry (son of the enemy) confronts Spiderman, (whom he now knows is Peter Parker). In response to Harry's accusation, Peter replies, "There are bigger things going on here than you or me." This salient thought should be considered, continually, as we decipher God's plan for our existence and attempt to comprehend things beyond the daily grind of life; a whole other level—a bigger picture—exists, "it's proper end."

So what are some of the 'bigger' things that have boggled the human brain for centuries? How does one create something—anything—from absolutely nothing? How do you create something invisible? Some of the invisible things of life include: air/wind; gravity; electromagnetic force; the strong and weak nuclear forces; consciousness and instinct. All are needed for life! Just because we can't fully grasp these "bigger things" doesn't mean we should ignore and not address them.

In regards to the spiritual dimension, we wonder if there is a heaven and a hell. Is there spiritual activity going on around us? Is there a divine life-plan in place that is reliable?

> How does one create something—anything—from absolutely nothing?

We have air, water and food which all 'magically' provide sustenance that is necessary for life. We even have senses to experience this incredibly complex world and communicate ideas with others. God made the sun for light, energy, regeneration and plant growth. These all prove that God wanted man to exist and thought of these things *prior* to the creation of Adam and Eve. Everything around us sustains our earthy bodies.

God is self sufficient. God had a great *desire* for our presence. Why did He desire for us to take part in His Creation, sharing the cosmos and consequently making His existence much more complicated? These questions arise from the mysteries of creation, and they are pertinent questions to cause wonder and to challenge us. God didn't give us answers directly for a reason. This huge, unfinished puzzle has been designed and created for us to discover and to glorify Him. One of the themes woven through the Bible is the notion of fellowship with God. He surely doesn't require our company; rather it is we who need Him. The relationship desired by God must be genuine. James 4: 4

> Since God is eternal, it stands to reason that He would not want the friendship to end upon our body's expiration.

> The devil's goal is to distract and deceive.

clearly states that there are two sides; we can choose to be a friend of God or to be His enemy. There is no middle ground. It is not unfair for God to want us to be on one side or the other because He gave us. . . everything! Since God is eternal, it stands to reason that *He would not want the friendship to end upon our body's expiration.* That would be a very brief and shallow relationship. His blueprint included an endless bond for eternity, inclusive of an everlasting body and soul:

> *So will it be with the resurrection of the dead. The body that is sown is perishable, it is raised imperishable; it is sown in dishonor, it is raised in glory; it is sown in weakness, it is raised in power; it is sown a natural body, it is raised a spiritual body. If there is a natural body, there is also a spiritual body.*

> I Cor. 15: 42–44 (NKJV)

shows
The Bible shoes us over and over that we are of the utmost importance to our Creator and He loves us completely. He allows distractions, trials and obstacles to test our faithfulness, to develop our character and. to humble or to teach us. When we discover why these events occurred, another puzzle piece is put into place.

To understand the trial puzzle piece, the Apostle Peter encouraged other Christians to be strong as the persecution of Christians spread throughout Asia:

> *These trials will show that your faith is genuine. It is being tested as fire tests and purifies gold—though your faith is far more precious than mere gold. So when your faith remains strong through many trials, it will bring you much praise and glory and honor on the day when Jesus Christ is revealed to the whole world.*

> I Peter 1: 7

The bible is filled with many stories of people who suffered tribulations, such as Job, Moses, David, Jonah and even God's own son. Trials can change our perspective and we usually grow and get to know God better working through these challenges.

These numerous distractions can be dangerous and are orchestrated by another conductor. God has allowed a fallen creation—the devil—to emerge and to assert tests that may have eternal ramifications. 2 Corinthians 11: 3, 1 Timothy 3: 7 and Daniel 8: 25 communicate that *the devil's goals are to distract, deceive and to destroy.* And he does this cunningly. Remember, the devil doesn't want us to solve our puzzle because with each placed piece, we are closer to seeing the completed picture.

Jesus explains that the enemy who sowed weeds in the farmer's field is a simile for the devil and his deeds. When we develop a correct perspective regarding how God uses our troubles, we can learn to be faithful to God and ourselves as His people. *The deceiver's work is invisible to our physical eyes* but recognizable (though not always immediately, like a weed's root system underground), through the discernment of the Holy Spirit within believers. The deceiver works to weaken our resolve and pushes believers to distrust God.

Another weapon of the devil is to distort our uniqueness. Our skin, hair, eyes, shape, and even our size can create fear. We often prejudge a person based on appearances. Unfortunately, wrong judgements are made as well based on disinformation. Satan is referred to as "the father of lies" in the book of John.

Many of us will be given eighty or more years on this planet, which is plenty of time to exercise our ability to make choices. The most important decision we can make is to spend some of those precious days thinking about the things of God. This choice may determine your eternal destination.

In fact, some have already decided to reject the things of God and God knows it! The Word of God states that the things of God are "foolishness to those that are perishing." These are difficult words to hear, but they are pertinent for understanding God's planning, "before the

> # Sin blocks us from discerning truth and, worst of all, it prevents us from getting to know God.

beginning." God is the ultimate playwright. He has put a spellbinding drama of good vs. evil into motion. The title of this very significant play—*Life*. He was already aware of those who would turn their backs on him before He even held the first casting call. He knew who would play the roles of the murderers, the thieves, the liars, and those whose lives would be consumed with hatred for his fellow man.

A question that plagues many is: How could a loving God allow such evil to happen in our world today?[5] Just *after* the beginning, in the Garden of Eden, everything was as God intended, existing in perfect peace and harmony. Sadly, Adam and Eve disobeyed God and chose evil, opening the porthole for the devil to slither into our world. We are all born with a sinful nature. If we don't accept that salient element of our personalities, ramifications are inevitable. Sin is very destructive and separates us from God. It's very hard for most of us to see sin as God sees it.

> *But your iniquities have made a separation between you and your God, And your sins have hidden His face from you so that He does not hear.*
>
> Isaiah 59: 2 (NKJV)

I look at sin as a wall, or a blockade. Sin interferes with our ability to have an abundant and full life. Sin blocks us from discerning truth and, worst of all, prevents us from getting to know God. Some of the names we have given these blockades include arrogance, pride and idolatry. These blockades act like an undetectable veil to eternal truths. They allow lies of every sort to distort who we are. The good news is that

these blockades can be discovered and exposed in our lives as we identify them. Once identified, we need to overcome these hurdles through
prayer and reading God's Word. This passage in Matthew is of great
help during this process:

> *But seek first His kingdom and His righteous-*
> *ness, and all these things will be added to you.*

Matthew 6: 33 (NKJV)

This intentional thinking on our part can launch blockade-busting
missiles to bring about change!

> *But we all, with unveiled face, beholding as in a mirror the*
> *glory of the Lord, are being transformed into the same im-*
> *age from glory to glory, just as by the Spirit of the Lord.*

II Corinthians 3: 18 (NKJV)

I mentioned earlier that God is the divine playwright. Let's jump to
the end of the play for a moment. After physical life has ended and all
of life's distractions (blockades) are set aside, we will be in eternity with
God. Understanding the very nature of God, being transcendent (set
apart from all that we know) in Holiness and all that is good. We will
find ourselves in the presence of a loving heavenly Father who cares
very deeply about us. He cares about the condition of our hearts now,
in the journey, and later when we are in His presence.

Awesome Minds

Since we are created in the image of God, can we have a mind similar
(in some teeny tiny respects) to His? I am awestruck when I think
about the mind of God. He had the incredible mental power to create
a human brain, with all of its marvelous complexities. What a design
challenge! The human brain is a highly technical and complex organ.
It can differentiate things, it can manage an entire central nervous

system and respond to all stimuli through sensory nerves for sight, sound, touch, speech, hearing, smell and my favorite. . . taste![6] With the brain, we are able to read, interpret and store information that is gathered from each of the nerve's senses. To be able to play back and transmit these stored memories/instructions to the appropriate body part is beyond amazing. Our brain gives instructions to our appendages. It runs our organs. The brain tells microbodies when and where there is an infection then sends an army of antibodies to the battleground to fight in the name of our health!

According to Dr. Swenson, within a single gram of brain tissue, "there are 400 billion synaptic junctions"[7] that conduct healing and bodily functions above and below our skin. These junctions provide a warning when something is too hot or too cold with our "450 sensory cells on each square inch of our skin."[8] This brain tissue, "with just under 200,000 miles of neurons and dendritic connections,"[9] has the ability to link information, which we call knowledge. Our minds allow us to be able to use that knowledge to create, teach, protect, feed, inform, lead, fight or flee. When we use our knowledge correctly, we call that wisdom. This gray matter with a "storage capacity equal to that contained in 25 million books"[10] also has the ability to discern, salivate, procrastinate, pursue, get happy, feel a dozen emotions and trigger a tear that communicates sadness. It can pick up multiple communication signals from others through words and through body language. A wink or roll of our eyes, a simple smirk, the raising of a single eyebrow, crossed arms, a lofty glance or a shoulder shrug all communicate in subtle ways. The brain is designed to be drawn to interests, to find a mate, to procreate, speculate, animate, formulate, differentiate, articulate, agitate, anticipate, appreciate or celebrate. And, each of our brains is designed to be unique from all of the other brains on the planet!

Our brain is designed with the ingenuity to create and invent on its own, to truly think independently, to problem solve, to fix, to build, to discover and to desire and seek adventure. We have the ability to conquer our fears and to take on different levels of risk. Our mind desires and enjoys a good story. It has the ability to create a story, and desires to know the conclusion.

The brain has to be housed in a safe place to protect it from everyday knocks, bumps and bruises. Hence, we have a skull. The brain tells us when to open and close our eyes and our mouth. It tells us when we are hungry and thirsty. It will even break down if not properly loved. Could there be a message to us here? Again, we are brought back to consider the bigger things that are tied to our ultimate friendship with God.

In fact, the Bible teaches that we have an emptiness *built inside* that can only be filled by God. We are truly mysteriously and wonderfully made! We have been created to love and be loved. As Augustine once said, "God has made us for Himself, and our hearts are restless until we find our rest in Him." Augustine, Confessions, 1.1.1. In the 43rd chapter of Isaiah, God claims His people:

> *Everyone who is called by My name, And*
> *whom I have created for My glory, Whom I*
> *have formed, even whom I have made.*

Is: 43: 7

Loving Us Through Design

There is a powerful God-given trait that we all possess. It is a vital attribute for reaching our full potential. For some, discovering it can drive them to levels of accomplishments they never believed they could achieve. For others, it can be a dangerous, all consuming monster that devours life in one gulp. Two men in the Bible who exemplify these extremes are Paul and David. Both possessed this trait in abundance, but at times their hearts were ruled by something as far from God as one can get. What is this God-given gift that can raise us up to new levels of understanding one day and, if we're not careful, cast us into the valley of destruction the next? It is passion.

Passion

Many would agree that ours is a God of passion. Webster defines passion as "an extreme, compelling emotion; an intense emotional drive or excitement; a great anger, rage, fury, enthusiasm, strong love or affection." A synonym for passion is the word zeal. According to BibleGateway.com, this word is in use anywhere from twice to 36 times, depending on the translation (King James, The Message, NIV, Wycliffe, etc). However, the word zeal is seldom used in modern language because it's an outdated word for modern conversations. Passion, like the word zeal, carries an intensity and depth in its meaning.

Other descriptive terms for the word passion include: "a strong, fervent desire, an ardent affection, enthusiastic devotion to a cause, ideal, or goal and tireless diligence in its furtherance."[11] There cannot be passion without *emotion*. When God said that He wished that "none would perish" there was great conviction and anguish behind those words. When the Lord's people were praising Jesus as He entered Jerusalem as a king, the Pharisees demanded that His disciples be quiet. Jesus replied that if the disciples kept silent, even the rocks would "cry out." One assumes that a "cry" contains great emotion, right? But how can rocks have emotion? The Lord personified an inanimate and seemingly useless object and gave it a human characteristic to make a point.

If lowly, useless rocks would cry out to praise the Lord in the Bible, what would other creations of God express? What would the majestic mountains and explosive oceans be saying if they could speak? What utterances of the glorious Creator would the trees and hills whisper? Whatever they would say, I believe their voices would be filled with *passion*!

> There is a powerful God-given trait that we all possess which is a vital attribute in reaching our fullest potential.

Because *we* are made in the image of God, He made our minds, hearts and souls *passion and compassion capable.* What an awesome trait, to be hardwired into our very core! No other trait permeates our being as passion does. And when God is behind

> What would the majestic mountains and explosive oceans be saying if they could speak?

the passion (in its truest sense), man can *move mountains*! Please see page 21 for passion clarification.

When we are impassioned, obstacles and excuses are reduced in size. We find ways to make big things happen. When we discover who God intended us to be—when we discover our purpose—we become focused and driven! Depressive tendencies vanish; excitement, and ultimately, true contentment, can replace it. In the book of John, Jesus said, "I am come that they might have life, and have it abundantly." Sadly, although we all possess this great gift, many of us inadvertently suppress it, hide it, or may even experience shame from it. I am afraid

> He made our minds, hearts and souls *passion capable.*

to be passionate at times, for fear of having my hopes and dreams smashed or dampened. Fear often comes from our inner self. It is not of God. Fear is an evil thing when the fear of failure rules our lives and prevents us from reaching our divine purpose.

Most of us have probably never given much thought about the *power* of passion, or the role that the Holy Spirit plays as we try to navigate the road of life. By yielding to the Holy Spirit, great things can be accomplished. If we are willing to define and let go of other distractions, blessings are sure to follow. Seeking the Lord *fervently* helps us discover all that God has in store for us.

In his book entitled *Primal*, Mark Batterson talks about the raw intensity needed in our approach to God—primal compassion, primal wonder, primal curiosity and primal energy.[12] Batterson goes on to say that souls are lost because of the lack of passion and enthusiasm—for a believer's soul.

David was a man after God's own heart, but David had a dark side. He was capable of first-degree murder. He had lust, not passion, in his heart that drove him to commit adulterous behavior with Bathsheba. David plotted well in advance to have Bathsheba's husband Uriah killed, to conceal his adulterous

> When we are impassioned, obstacles and excuses seem to reduce in size.

affair. However, David also had a thoughtful and curious side. Reading the words of remorse that David later recorded in the pages of the Bible, we can see that he easily expressed his emotions, attitudes and interests. David took the time to repent. He took the time to praise, worship and think deeply about God. Scholars believe David wrote 73 songs of praise in the book of Psalms.[13] Many have inspired worship songs that are still being sung in churches today—over 3,000 years later!

Paul, as Saul, murdered scores of Christians, with zeal. However, one day God struck him with lightening and took his sight away.

> Why would God overlook such vile behavior and still use mankind in great ways?

Finally, after Paul considered the things that Jesus had said to Him, Paul's sight was returned to him and he was transformed. Later, Paul led many people to a saving relationship with Jesus as Lord. He was filled with such conviction that he was glad to be imprisoned for his beliefs. He authored several letters that are now part of the New Testament and continue to inspire many believers through his incredible witness and devotion.

Why would God overlook such vile behavior and still use mankind in great ways? Through these stories, we see how God loves us even when we are buried under mountains of character flaws. He sees our potential! God is showing us that He can use anyone He chooses; even you and me!

The Lord is compassionate and gracious,
slow to anger, abounding in love.
⁹ He will not always accuse,
nor will he harbor his anger forever;
¹⁰ He does not treat us as our sins deserve
or repay us according to our iniquities.
¹¹ For as high as the heavens are above the earth,
so great is His love for those who fear him;
¹² as far as the east is from the west,
so far has He removed our transgressions from us.
¹³ As a father has compassion on his children,
so the Lord has compassion on those who fear Him;
¹⁴ for He knows how we are formed,
He remembers that we are dust.

Psalm 103: 8–14 (NIV)

> When God said to love Him with all of our heart, mind and strength, He expected us do it passionately.

Man was granted the gift of passion by God, but man is obviously influenced by self and the enemy. David lusted after Bathsheba and committed murder. Saul, a Pharisee under Jewish law, was zealous enough to persecute the early church, even to the point of taking lives. Through the working of the Holy Spirit, and God, Paul and David were transformed. They lived life to the fullest, according to God's will, rather than their own. God saw this and was pleased.[14] He set David and Paul apart and never left each man's side.

An example of a modern day Godly man of passion leads a small Tennessee based church. However, he has a large and growing social media following. What I love about this man is not only does he know scripture extremely well but fear isn't in his vocabulary. Well at least fear of his fellow man.

When the Pastor gets fired up on the fails of mankind, he rips into it with everything he's got. He's not worried about who he is going to offend, or upset, who might leave the church or quit tithing. His words are spot on and in your face. The passion he exhibits is evident in his calling. I've seen him sob, grieve and in elation, bounce around the alter like a pinball bouncing off rubber bumpers. He is animated, humourous and cutting through the mundane to reach hearts. I am sure there are others and I am happy to take note of them as I become aware.

When a message hits to the core, especially when an audience is not ready to accept the truth, the initial reaction can be upsetting. The pastor gets threatened, mocked, laughed at, and criticized. False accusations flow like a river because the ungodly hate when their deeds are exposed. This Pastor is an inspiration to me because he is engaged with his God-given talents. It is evident the man loves God. He has been given gifts of charisma and wisdom and he's working it to the glory of our Creator. Another trait is that he listens to the Holy Spirit. Many times he believes he has to stop what he's doing and preach a 3 minute sermon because he knows someone discouraged and/or depressed needs to hear that message immediately. God is indeed raising him up to do an incredible work.

Dr. Jobe Martin, DDS is another example of a passionate Godly man. Dr. Martin has written many resources detailing the handiwork of God in the creation of animals. He communicates the love of God exhibited through the design of God's creation.

> Paul and David were transformed and lived their lives *passionately* in a new way.

Dr. Martin talks simply about animals with unique characteristics. He pushes us beyond traditional thinking about such things.

Dr. Martin is standing up to a culture steeped into a scientific account of earth's origins. To do this takes courage, fortitude and passion.

There are many animals that challenge man intellectually, some directly and some indirectly. Dr. Martin covers several of these in his material. When we focus on the animals with characteristics that are inherently designed with a message, lesson, example or a practical observation, we are blessed with new insight. It becomes strongly apparent that a great 'dad-like' God and a 'dad-like' designer—is intimately behind all that we see! Recognition of this intimacy brings glory to God. Chapter seven highlights nine animals that are very complex in design, yet simply amazing.

The late Steve Irwin, crocodile hunter and wildlife warrior exhibited an extreme passion working with animals. A interview with Steve's wife revealed that when Steve was with animals, nothing else mattered! He was focused, in love and steeped in mission. For Irwin, crocodiles represented dinosaurs that were not extinct but left for us to discover, study and wonder about. Steve wanted to preserve and protect crocs as well as many other animals.[16] Irwin's family didn't sweat the small stuff. It was in their genes to get dirty, wet and engaged. Animals can be dirty, wet and very exciting! Steve's example of engagement with creation remains an inspiration to me.

When we look at God's creations, considering the lilies, it can take our worship to a deeper level, because we begin to think about the fact that there is a loving and caring God behind it all.

God designed us. He can use us, even though we are weak and far from perfect. He intentionally designed us this way in order to accomplish His will. He can love us through our unique design. We are a part of His story. We are called to live life *passionately*! When God said to love Him with all of our heart, mind and strength, He expected us to do it passionately. Passion is the greater good over suffering and sacrifice.

The Angst of Passion

The word passion is full of angst because it has the power to defeat the enemy's work. Attempting to describe the creating power of God is daunting to say the least. However, having phrasing that brings us part way there, can help to communicate what He has done and is doing for us. My best shot at describing the creating power of God is this:

> The Holy Spirit engaged is passion. This passion births life, hope and purpose. It can heal the original wound inflicted in the Garden. The Holy Spirit is like a fire; He brings God's presence, God's power, and God's purity together. Passion is not lust or love-making but can create life. Passion is not selfish ambition but a pursuit of restoration. Passion is not stagnant or will-less, it engages and rescues. Passion is not a spectator but it watches with care, it watches you.

God demonstrated His love to us through creation. Like many words, the meaning of passion can change depending on it's context. There are two particular over-riding views that will dictate its context: God's point of view or man's point of view.

First: God is omniscient, all knowing and outside of time.

> The word passion is full of angst because it has the power to defeat the enemy's work.

He knew that His free agents, Adam and Eve, would choose wrongly in the Garden. Did the sin of disobedience, which caused separation from God, create a wound that needed healing? Yes, the relationship was broken. Man was now on his own, no longer walking side-by-side with God, and left to self-manage, until God would bring a way of restoration. **Before the beginning, God was thinking about restoration.** God uses creation to reveal Himself to man. Creation makes us wonder, it is intriguing, always revealing something new and astounding. It offers life-sustaining perfection interwoven with symbiosis, all passionately created for us to look to Him. Creation unveils the bigness of God and His love and passion for us.

> Creation unveils the bigness of God and His love and passion for us.

Second: From man's viewpoint, God's instructions to us are clear. We are to love God with all our heart, mind and strength. We have an evil adversary who has one objective—stop the restoration. The enemy will use all kinds of unthinkable snares. Present and generational curses will confound and cripple, leaving us for physical and spiritual death. Satan's demonic ranks are focused in their mission. Should we yield, unspeakable torments are certain. Sober thinking will conclude that a fight for life is at hand. A reckoning of personal weakness will need to take place—a need for knee and heart bowing humility.[17]

> For what I am doing, I do not understand; for I am not practicing what I would like to do, but I am doing the very thing I hate.
>
> Romans 7: 15:

This fight of a lifetime will have to emerge from a place within, where spirit and soul reside. The power source of the Holy Spirit will drive the fight. Once the will is infused with divine energy, the resulting passion will put the King of kings *first* in our surrendered lives. It takes inspired infused passion for authentic transformation to take place.

> As the deer pants for the water brooks, So
> my soul pants for You, O God.
>
> Psalm 42: 1

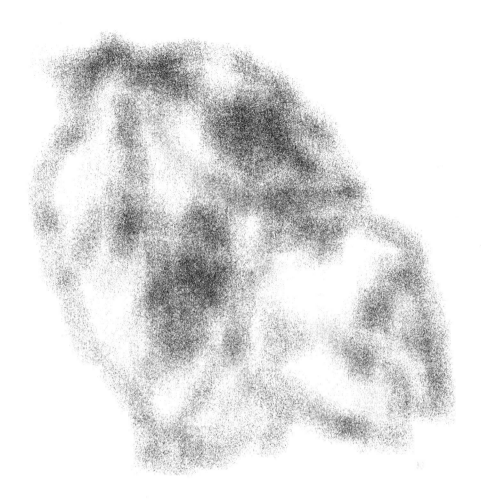

2

God's Heart in Communication With Man's Heart

Michelangelo's painting of God's hand reaching to touch man's hand is quite astonishing, especially once you learn about one other element of the painting. In the background, behind God, there is a slightly cam-ouflaged shape of a brain! According to the guide at the Sistene Chapel, this is believed to represent the mind of God. Michelangelo's talent (like that of Beethoven, Bach and others) was so unique and beautiful that it has been difficult to fully credit him alone as the beginning and end of

Michelangelo's, *The Creation of Adam*, fresco painting.

his work. These artists works have been widely recognized as divinely inspired.

The Word of God is inspired. If the Bible is not *your* final authority, or at least highly respected in your mind's eye, then this chapter's title "God's Heart in Communication With Man's Heart" weakens greatly in its significance. If you are not sure about authenticity, then take it "on faith" that just maybe, its origin is God's heart, then the words will have a much greater chance to reach the core of your being.

We are His children and He longs for us. Those of us who are parents know the love we feel toward our children. We long for them. We enjoy the wonderful feeling of holding our children in our arms. They ride perfectly on our forearms as newborns. A toddler sits neatly on a mother's hip; the fit is perfect!

The bond between parents and children is so precious. God desires this same intimate bond with us! When parents see their own characteristics (such as dad's sense of humor or mom's compassion towards others) in their own children, these parent-child connections are good for the soul. When God sees the spirit of His own attributes reflected in His children, He is pleased. Scripture addressed the depth of God's longing for this in the book of James:

He jealously desires the Spirit which He has made to dwell in us.

James 4: 5

Can you imagine having this as a design challenge? In His desire to make a brain capable of feeling connected, God met and surpassed His goal! Wow! Our brains are designed to "feel connected" to our loving Father and that is such a wonderful thing!

As I mentioned earlier, we were designed with feelings and emotions as a central core of our being. Some argue that our emotions are what separate us from the animal kingdom; that they are what make us "human." But many animal lovers will disagree with that reasoning. We can probably agree on a few things about this aspect of who we are: Feelings complicate life. They can be fickle and mislead us at times. When someone speaks to us about certain things, emotions can be difficult to read. We sort out the feelings of others by picking up on things like facial expressions, body language and voice tone. There are also clues to understanding God's heart.

> The bond between parents and children is so precious. God desires this same intimate bond with us!

> In His desire to make a brain capable of feeling connected, God certainly met His goal!

We see hundreds of references to man's heart in the Bible. Yet, it is somewhat amazing that there are few references to God's heart. Only 26 of 598 references to heart in the Old Testament allude to God's heart.[1] However, we are continually encouraged to *know* God. The book of Psalms advises that we come to know Him through His law, commands, statutes, precepts and decrees. Many of these refer to our approach to God and we may use references to build a foundation of divine understanding. Through the Scriptures, we can begin to comprehend the heart of God.

The Lion Witch and the Wardrobe is a movie based upon the series of books by Christian author, C. S. Lewis. In the story, Mr. Tumnus, a mythical fawn, is befriended by Lucy one of the young protagonists. Mr. Tumnus tries to explain to Lucy the comings and goings of Aslan the Lion, a symbolic Christ figure in the story. He tells her, "After all He is not a tame lion." It is difficult for Lucy to grasp this new world with such a unique king, who is so cherished. Similarly, Proverbs 3: 5-6 states, "In all your ways acknowledge Him, lean not on your own understanding." Though it may be a challenge to love Him, who we do not always understand, this is what we are called to do. Philippians 3:10 reads, "That I may *know* Him, and the power of His resurrection . . ." These verses invite us to intimately know Him with all of our being and to rely on God and His Word, rather than our own understanding. This is where the amazing faith-walk begins. By leaning on His promise, and by letting go of our human understanding, we can learn to fully and wholeheartedly believe that God loves us completely. Through the stories in the Bible, we see His compassion, mercy, loving kindness, and the ultimate gift and sacrifice of His Son, Jesus. It is the unspoken message to our hearts, that the heart of God is very good, indeed.

Let me understand the teachings of your precepts!
Then I will meditate on your wondrous works.

Psalm 119: 27 (NHM)

The Message

In 1990 during a heart-wrenching trial of survival in my graphics career, my Pastor came to me and said, "Jim, I do not know what this means and I have never had this happen before, but in my sleep, I believe the Holy Spirit told me to tell you that He cares more for the condition of your heart than the condition of your business." For two years, my workload slid down to the point where I was no longer able to support my family. Although this happened over 20 years ago, I have never forgotten his words. It didn't have the depth of meaning then as it does today. Through our intense trials, and in times of reflection, I have been overwhelmed by questions that refer to the "condition of my heart." Did I lose perspective because I chose the value of my business over of the value of my heart? Yes indeed! Paying attention to what makes us tick, is a good idea.

Biblically, King Solomon, considered the wisest man to ever live, gives us a stern warning in Proverbs 4:23. He says, "Above all else, guard your heart, for it is the wellspring of life." Protecting our heart ranks high with God. Why did King Solomon say this? A state of innocence was given to us before the fall of Adam and Eve. We are designed to make the choices which show the genuineness of our friendship with God. Also, it's good to learn from these lessons and tests. As we do, it becomes easier to grow spiritually as a child of God. More of life's puzzle pieces begin to fit together.

During times of trial, we were dealt crushing blows financially. In the field of communications, when signs indicate the economy is declining, industries cut advertising dollars. When the economy improves, advertising is usually the last to be restored. Contacts in this field can be quite transient. You have to keep reselling yourself. Then there is the ever-changing software! Our local paper quoting me in their quote of the month. I stated that the economic slowdown was caused by everyone trying to learn their new software program, not a reduction in factory orders, the usual reason for a turndown in the 80's and 90's. In such situations, it's easy to lose sight of the fact that I am a child of the King. Financial worries are very devastating to believers and non-believers alike. People have even taken their lives when they feel they have no way out. I know what it's like to have my back against the wall and to live with the frustration of not being able to pay bills on time and with the thought of bankruptcy looming overhead. It's a very tough place to be. But today, I rejoice in the fact that I used the tools described in the Bible to survive, to keep myself literally alive! One of the verses that I hung onto then (and now) is. . .

For I am confident of this very thing, that He who began a good work in you will perfect it until the day of Christ Jesus.

Philippians 1: 6

This verse reminds me of the intimate involvement of a loving father. Because I lost the presence of my earthly father through divorce at an early age, the Creator's great love for me has made a tremendous impact in my life today.

God says that there is vulnerability, weakness, and a tendency to drift away from His special and divine plan for us. Philippians 4:6, another survival verse, tells us not to worry about anything, but to bring our prayers before the Lord. And if we do so, the "peace of God will guard your hearts and minds in Christ Jesus." What a delightful message we are given here! The passage indeed infers that God has a passionate desire to safekeep His creation. Do we need safekeeping? Absolutely! When our hearts are broken, we feel it.

> God originally wired us to be *heart sensitive* and to, in essence, to be our brother's keeper.

In fact, if we are not grounded in a relationship with the Lord, our life course may be completely derailed. Sometimes, we are able to muster the willpower to get back on track, and other times, God's sends someone to help us out. I am learning to manage these healthy concerns.

The *Andy Griffith Show* was popular in the 1960s and 1970s. (A heart felt thank you goes out to Andy and the producers for their work. Andy is now present with the Lord). Viewers were swept away by the nostalgia of the small town of Mayberry, North Carolina and all of the memorable characters that lived and worked there. Barney Fife, Otis, Ernest T. Bass, Goober, Aunt Bee and Opie were all colorful characters, but it was the sheriff, Andy Taylor, who always had a kind word (usually based on a biblical principal) to steer folks back to the right path. Everyone looked to the sheriff to rescue them from daily dilemmas and to make sure everyone was safe and sound. Andy had a way of caring for others in a warm and tender manner that no one else possessed. This was truly the "feel good" show of the era. Sometimes, it may seem as though these characteristics have all but disappeared in this world of climbing corporate ladders and keeping up with the Jones.' But God originally wired us to be *heart sensitive* and to, in essence, be our brother's keeper.

> If a thought about God warms your heart, comforts you, directs you, convicts you, teaches you, or makes you question or dig deeper, God is pleased. His motive is to lead us to Him.

As God developed the story of Life (with a capitol L), He was careful to involve all facets of great drama: a great story line, conflict and resolution, with both internal and external conflict. In our world, there is good and evil, beauty and ugliness, truth and deception. The saga of Life has depth and breadth, and it is filled with mystery and intrigue. But, as in all stories, there is a message.

In fact, God doesn't have just one message, but an eternity of messages. Some are big picture items that involve our destiny,

> In the concept of communication, there are only three elements: a sender, a receiver and a message.

step-by-step, through choices that we make. Some messages are small, but still significant. If a thought with God in mind warms your heart, comforts you, directs you, convicts you, teaches you, or makes you question and dig deeper, God is pleased. After all, His design gave us inquisitive minds. His motive is to lead us to Him.

> *After you have suffered for a little while, the God of all*
> *grace, who called you to His eternal glory in Christ, will*
> *Himself perfect, confirm, strengthen and establish you.*

> I Peter 5: 10

In the concept of communication, there are only three elements: a sender, a receiver and a message. God invites us to speak to Him through prayer, and He craves one-on-one time "without ceasing," according to chapter 5 of Thessalonians. Yet, when it comes to communicating with God, many fail. We are responsible for a breakdown in the communication process, because we stubbornly refuse to access the power that can come through prayer. We miss out on guidance, strength, healing and hope. He makes it very easy. He simply says to pray and our loving Father will hear our songs of rejoicing and cries of remorse. He is patiently waiting to hear from us.

> *But know that the LORD has set apart the godly man for*
> *Himself; The LORD hears when I call to Him.*

> Psalm 4: 3

What does our heart need to hear—or perhaps experience—when we cross the plane from the physical world into the spiritual world via this amazing communication line? When my son was five, he would come to my wife and me for a morning hug. He did this with no encumbrances; he just purely desired to feel close to us. This loving act was placed in my son for me to cherish. Even today, I treasure this memory.

When I was a toddler, I remember climbing in bed just wanting to be close to my parents and my dad getting very angry because of this. I remember leaving and being a little heart-broken. Today, I really don't blame him, because there were five of us kids, and he needed his space. However, it did hurt me to be unable to seek comfort in this way.

My son's morning hugs brought a healing message of acceptance and comfort. This is a great illustration of the way God wants us to work within the communication model: We enter His presence and send the message that we need to feel loved. He receives our message and responds by drawing us closer to Him. It's that simple.

I know that a father's rejection may not be a significant life-hurt to some, however, these events shouldn't be ignored as God can use whatever He chooses to reach our hearts.

A more significant example of how God ministered to my heart was during *another* economic downturn. Real estate holdings, stocks, savings, all materially was lost. As an artist/designer, I am somewhat sensitive to things. I continually examine myself. If you are a creative person, you may understand that sensitivity can be wired into our DNA. It can be a gift but can also be a curse. Door after door was being closed in the graphics field. The battle of self-worth begins once again! In an effort to seek work my resume was redesigned and sent to the multitudes. I was met with very few replies. Was it the economy? Had my abilities become outdated? Round and round I went! The painful burden of questions plagued my brain, day and night! The mental anguish and frustration wouldn't go away. It felt like death by a thousand cuts.

Suicide is on the rise, and now I can see why. Loss is devastating, it's easy to take it personaly and simultaneously loose *all* sense of hope. God is about hope. Our country's leaders have been removing Judeo/Christian values at every turn. Many have been distracted away from things of God, the source of hope. Yielding to ungodly things of the world.

If there is not a turn personally and/or culturally, our new norm will be what we are experiencing, a rise in soul-grabbing evil. By the way, if you are in a zombie-like, spiritual coma or painfully perplexed, then maybe it's time to ask, "why is this happening to me Lord?—help me to *hear* you."

If My people who are called by My name will humble themselves, and pray and seek My face, and turn from their wicked ways, then I will hear from heaven, and will forgive their sin and heal their land.

II Chronicles 7: 14 (NKJV)

Finally, I stopped and asked God what I was missing. It then occurred to me that I had not fulfilled the plan that I made with God for our new house. I was to use the house for *His* work. I hurried back to the *Before the Beginning* manuscript. Finally, after months of oppressive anguish, I understood: I wasn't giving my *full attention* to His call.

To my amazement and shock, two chapter outlines that I had started five years earlier were what we had just spent four years doing in farming! These chapters were titled, "The Beasts About" and "The Garden Around Us." When I had started those chapters we had no idea how we would use our property. I believe that God wanted us to experience specific details of His handiwork that Jesus used in His parables and teachings so I could write the chapters in relevant detail.

> Finally, I understood: I wasn't giving my *full attention* to His call.

My entire being has been worn out from all the uncertainty that I felt was raining down on my life. I was asking daily, when will the unrelenting pain end?

God knew of my depleted state. Mercy began to engage. My wife went on a timely weekend trip to Washington D.C. with a dear friend. It turned out that our friend knew the creation researcher who was a national broadcaster for Moody Bible Institute. I realized that nothing happens by coincidence! I asked the researcher if he would consider taking a look at the book that I wrote which was certainly inspired by his work. We had a common desire: to bring to light God's genius as both Creator *and* Designer. He responded by writing a very warm review for my book. God knew that *this* would minister to me and lift my heart. I am eternally grateful that God lovingly cares for the condition of my heart.

God shares His love with us through others in countless ways. He can use creation likewise. A timely breeze during a heart-felt prayer, a parting of clouds to hold back rain, a squirrel darting about the yard to entertain us, and a noble canine rescue are just a few of a many ways our God can communicate through creation. *In The Likeness of God*, written by Dr. Paul Brand and Philip Yancey, spiritual metaphors are brought to life to give testimony to our creator in great detail. One of the book's messages is that ours is a thoughtful God who *carefully integrated love into His Creation* for us to experience.

> God shares His love with us through others in countless ways.

If turbulence abounds in your life, then you might find a soothing message in a simple cat's purr, a gentle, steady rain or a comforting breeze across your skin. Did you know that cats only purr around humans and not with other cats? If inconsistency or instability plays a part in your life, then the faithfulness of a trusting canine may serve you well.

A friend of the family took a hedgehog into her care. She didn't expect to be so enamored with it. She said that once you get past the flesh-piercing spikes you can enjoy it! The noise that came from it is so bizarre that it reminded her of a children's wind-up toy. The hedgehog also reminded her of the wildness and humor that God designed into this creature. It makes us crack up! (This friend introduces children to the creation process through teaching the subject of art.)

> Would a "message" from God's heart to your heart make a difference?

Would a "message" from God's heart to your heart make a difference? What crevice would it fill or what need would it meet? Perhaps the message is purely cerebral, solving a life-puzzle of sorts. There might be a matter that weighs upon your heart and leaves you in pain or distress. God is standing by, just waiting to hear from you. A Psalmist writes, "His shadow is cast over our right hand."

> When was the last time you prayed for your heart?

When was the last time you prayed for your heart? Has it become embittered, timid, or broken? Whatever the state, God wants our hearts to be *near the place* where He originally created us! God wants us to have a contented heart, not choked by the worries of the world[2] or fretting about the next day or moment. Remember, God is the author of our hearts. He created every detail of you and me, including a beautiful mind, an amazing body and a spirit of peace. God communicates to us through our hearts.

The Ultimate Design Challenge!

Only in God's divine wisdom could an entire physiological human communication system be designed that performs the amazing tasks required of us every minute of every day.

> Only in God's divine wisdom could and entire physiological human communication system be designed which performs the amazing tasks required of us every minute of every day.

From God's perspective, He had to invent hearing. A listening system within the ears and brain. Sounds that not only trigger appropriate receptors, but receptors that permeate to our very core, our soul and heart. God invented the listening system complete with an eardrum, cochlea, and nerve-paths wired to the exact part of the brain with little "radar dishes" attached to our heads to catch the sound waves. He even gave us two!

The whole vocal cord noise-making and speech system has just the right amount of tension, attached to just the right place above the windpipe; even the larynx is an incredible thing. It needs constant lubrication to maintain consistency. This awesome piece of anatomy can create a variety of differentiating sounds, volumes, pitches and intonations. The vocal cords, along with the language forming tongue, cheeks and lips, are gloriously wired to a brain that is language competent and multilingual capable.

Every vocal cord comes complete with a range of tones, The user adjusts the tones by spontaneous thought. The vocal cords can create gentle tones that soothe a child or can shout a cheer at a baseball game. The cords were built to receive subtle signals from the brain that allow emotions to be expressed.

What do you think of a Designer God who equipped us so communication efficient?

The voice is amazing! Some of the tones and attitudes of expression include; caring, obnoxious, neutral, firm, coy, sneaky, mean, evil, nice, bored, excited, in love, out of love, happy, sad, angry, fearful, contemplative, pensive, interested, curious, encouraging, nurturing and flirtatious. In addition to talking, we are able to express our emotions, melodically in song! If you have ever been moved by a song or someone's voice, God is the real sound engineer behind it!

A really fascinating part of our noise making system is high tech sound effects! Childhood wouldn't be the same if we couldn't communicate in grunts, groans and coos. As our sound effects system develops we can make a plethora of sounds including motor-powered transportation, like a jet taking off or an old car engine starting up. From cooing at a newborn to speaking many languages, our vocal system is unbelievably versatile!

God invented lips that have the ability to press-together. Add some humming, and a tugboat becomes a speedboat. Go to a high-pitch hum and we have just added a 50 horsepower motor! Now reduce the lip pressure and you've instantly changed your sound effect from a speedboat to a motorcycle! Take a breath while making these sounds and you've just shifted gears—all for auditory fun and amusement!

Lips are a very important part of our portable sound effect studio. Lips are necessary to form different sounds. What's life without a whistle? Our lips, along with facial expression show a fireworks range of emotions: laughing, crying, and smiling. Our lips, together with our mouth and throat, allows us to mimic our animal friends by growling, barking, purring, mooing, quacking, squeaking, chattering and blowing fish bubbles. And some say our Creator doesn't have a sense of humor.

Not only is God's heart in communication with ours but He has given us the ability to be extremely creative in expressing ourselves with others. God values clear, on-point communication, especially when He uses others to send a message.

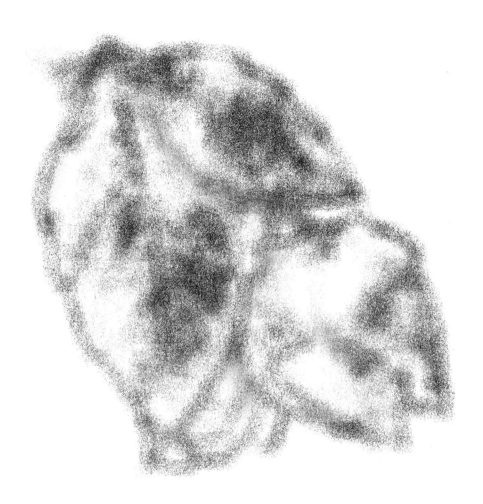

3
Inspirations of God

Where did God begin? He had no palette, no drawing board, no paper or pencil; there were no reference books, no "how-to" books, no internet to search, no Pinterest, no inspiration of any sort to draw upon. There was absolutely...nothing! How do we even wrap our minds around "nothing"? God didn't have a collection of molecules, atoms, electrons, protons or DNA to start with. He had to invent these microstructures first with all their abilities to interact and react with one-another before He could get into bigger things! There were no beakers, burners, scopes, measuring devices, no computers or modeling software, no chemicals or or-

> To help us understand God's creation process, we need to understand what *nothing* is.

ganic materials to work with. If we were to try and breakdown "nothing" into a mathematical equation, it might look like this.

$$(-\infty) + (+\infty) = (\quad)$$

I can't even use a "0" between the parentheses because zero is a number! I am not a mathematician in any way, but even I can understand this. From our earthly point of view, God's starting point for creation was ( ). According to Genesis 1:2 it was formless and void and dark. Our finite minds can only grasp "nothing" through the understanding of "something". After God went from "nothing" to the creation of the earth, sky, sea, and animals—He created us—in His own image. We are the crowning touch of His creation. We are above all the rest because we are like Him! We are created with a

> God didn't even have a collection of molecules, atoms, electrons, protons or DNA as a starting point.

soul and consciousness; we are created to think!

Contemplate this for a moment—what does it take to generate a single thought? According to a MIT School of Engineering article written by Elizabeth Dougherty, "Trying to imagine how trillions of connections and billions of simultaneous transmissions coalesce inside your brain to form a thought is a little like trying to look at the leaves, roots, snakes, birds, ticks, deer—and everything else in a forest—at the same moment."[1]

In the same article, Charles Jennings, director of neurotechnology at the MIT McGovern Institute for Brain Research tells us that "The human brain is composed of about 100 billion nerve cells (neurons) interconnected by trillions of connections, called synapses. On average, each connection transmits about one signal per second. Some specialized connections send up to 1,000 signals per second. 'Somehow... that's producing thought',"

What does it take to generate a single thought?

That's pretty mind-boggling. Think of all the movements your body makes without you even thinking about it. As I type this, I am not consciously telling my fingers to move over the keyboard, but my mind is doing just that at hyper speed! What kind of power does it take to push the detailed movement of my fingers typing through my body to my muscles in a split second? Our God knows!

The psalmist, when considering God's thoughts said this:

How precious to me are your thoughts, O God! How vast is the sum of them! Were I to count them, they would outnumber the grains of sand—when I awake, I am still with you.

Psalm 139: 17–18 (NIV)

I asked Dr. Jason Lyle, astronomer and physicist at the Institute of Creation Research, if he could estimate the number of grains of sand on the earth. He estimated "10^{22} (ten billion trillion total grains, give or take a factor of ten or so."[2] With that number divided into 7 billion (the number of people on the planet), that gives us plus or minus 10%, 1.4 trillion grains of sand per person. What an inconceivable number of thoughts directed toward each of us from God! Yes, this may simply be a figurative use of language, but two concepts are vast yet very clear—God never, EVER stops thinking about us. The original design of creation took into account everything that is required to sustain every form of life. Every single thing had to be thought of and engineered in perfect symbiotic balance and life-sustaining order—and to think that God just spoke all of this into existence. No more, no less. Divine design, engineering, authorship, and thought existed before time, it exists today, and it is everlasting:

> # Our God has a complete and thorough understanding of the molecular—He created it!

> *Before the mountains were born or you brought forth the earth*
> *and world, from everlasting to everlasting you are God.*
>
> Psalm 90: 2 (BSB)

God made us in His image and granted us the ability to think and to contemplate what thinking is. God also gave us the ability to create lesser things. Because of this, we can get a faith-building glimpse of the Creator of greater things.

> *Many, O LORD my God, are the wonders, which You*
> *have done, And Your thoughts toward us; there is none*
> *to compare with You. If I would declare and speak of them, they*
> *would be too numerous to count.*
>
> Psalm 40: 5

Scripture teaches that God holds all things together. Science teaches that there is a force that surrounds protons and atoms. The name that has been given to this phenomenon is called the Strong Force.[3] Science recognizes the invisible but can't always entirely explain it. Like human consciousness; it's there, but it cannot be completely explained. The mysteries of creation are infinite and unexplainable; Isaiah 55: 8 reads, "For my thoughts are not your thoughts and neither are your ways my ways, declares the Lord."

> Every single thing had to be thought of and engineered in perfect symbiotic balance and life sustaining order.

Technology is advancing our ability to see what's far away even if it's right under our noses. We can now view galaxies light years away and see the structure of each scale of a butterfly's wing. Each discovery should bring us closer to the one who's infinite, unfathomable creative design continues to show us intricate order and purpose.

As we can observe, God reveals Himself through creation. These are the blessings that work in sync with His Word. For example, verses like Psalm 19: 1 which reads, "The heavens declare the glory of God..." affirm our hope and strengthen our faith. With a telescope, we can see colorful Nebulas in the night sky. The hydrogen, gas and dust formation follows the spiral design pattern. This pattern is found in a mathematical sequence called the "Golden Ratio."[4] It's invisible in theory, bar a few math equations that represent it, but it's very visible in nature. You can see it in plants, pineapples and pinecones. Walking on the beach you can spot the spiral in seashells, snails and storms. The natural spiral pattern is easily recognized. When designers use a spiral as a pattern to follow, it creates natural flow and organization—something we have come to expect. When something strays from this foundational pattern, it becomes noticeable. God seems to have written it into our DNA. When a floral arrangement or work of art strays from the natural design order, it can look odd or displeasing to us. We sense that something is "off" about it.

The "Golden Ratio" shows us balance and beauty and order.

> God also gave us the ability to create lesser things. Because of this, we can get a faith-building glimpse of the Creator of greater things.

I mentioned some of the ways we apply this ratio, but I would like to take it a step further. Think about the traditional watch spring. For the watch to function properly the spring must be tightly wound—but not too tight or it will break. It has

> Is His power or even His physical presence closer to us than we realize?

to be wound daily to create a tension to power the watch. Just as like the watch spring, God uses stressors and tension in our lives to push us, grow us, and empower us. These are the things that make us into the image of Christ.

God's Heart

1 John 4:16 tells us that God is love. It is difficult to imagine that we could have any kind of impact on the heart of God, but the Bible indicates that we can grieve the heart of God.[5] Why would God create us, knowing that we would grieve His heart? It says in Genesis 1: 27 that God created us in His image. He wanted us to know the joy of fellowship with Him. He was not lonely, and He did not need us; instead He wanted to share His joy and love with us. In fact, as we see in creation—He wanted to shower us with His love!

> Many answers to the questions which perplex us lie in the invisibles of life.

In 1 John 3:1 (NIV) John exclaims, "See what great love the Father has lavished on us, that we should be called children of God"!

How can we bring joy instead of grief to God's heart? Psalm 37: 4 tells us, "Delight yourself in the LORD, and He will give you the desires of your heart." The Bible continually tells us that God wants us to turn our hearts towards Him, and by doing that He will reveal His love, compassion, faithfulness, and peace.

As parents, we can delight ourselves in our children. God has given us these parent-child relationships to learn and help us understand our relationship with Him. We see our children grow, learn, laugh and cry while our interest never wanes. In many ways, God's relationship to us is very similar to these relationships with our children. We are His children—growing and learning to look to Him. I can't believe how many times I have repeated to my children, "Would you just trust me"? I am prodded today as an adult with the same admonition from the Holy Spirit; in our moments of doubt and despair, He asks us, "Would you just trust me"?

Man's Heart

According to Jeremiah 17: 9, "The heart is more deceitful than all else and is desperately sick; who can understand it"?

As sons and daughters of Adam and Eve, we are prone to sin. We are often full of bitterness, envy, anger, unforgiveness and resentment. Bitterness, we are told, grows like a root and infects the whole body. Unforgiveness is one of the major reasons that people frequent therapists. In anger we can hurt someone physically and emotionally. Envy can give us hearts of ingratitude. All of these things harm our relationships with each other and with God our Father. If we try to wrestle with these issues alone, it will choke the life right out of us (Luke 8: 14). This is why we are called to bring all things to God in prayer. "Be anxious for nothing, but in everything, by prayer and petition, with thanksgiving, present your requests to God" (Philippians 4: 6, BSB).

And in 1 John 1: 9, we are told "If we confess our sins, he is faithful and just to forgive us our sins and to cleanse us from all unrighteousness." The Lord goes on to admonish us to "Be kind to one another, tenderhearted, forgiving one another, as God in Christ forgave you" (Ephesians 4: 32).

It is by confession, prayer and forgive-

> So what is it that motivated God to call us into existence?

ness of others, that we find peace, encouragement, and forgiveness for ourselves. This is how we weed out that root of bitterness and how our anger can be turned to gentleness and our envy to thankfulness. This is how God transforms our hearts into the image of Christ. As our hearts and minds are transformed, we find that peace that surpasses all under-

> I can't believe how many times I have repeated to my children, "Would you just trust me?"

standing, and that peace, in turn, will guard our hearts and minds in Christ Jesus (Philippians 4: 7). God's forgiveness allows us to be able to rest and let go so we can get a tiny glimpse into the tranquility of Heaven; a little bit of heaven on earth. That glimpse is nothing compared to what we will experience when we pass from this life into the next.

> *Eye has not seen, nor ear heard, nor have entered*
> *into the heart of man the things which*
> *God has prepared for those who love Him.*
>
> 1 Corinthians 2: 9 (NKJV)

We are told in 2 Corinthians 5: 8 that to be "absent from the body is to be present with the Lord." When Christ was hung on the cross as a sacrifice for our sins, He looked over to the thief who was on a cross next to him and said, "Today you will be with me in Paradise." Other verses tell us about a great banquet that will be served. It will be a time of celebration! Once we are in God's presence, life will finally be complete. Our hearts and spirits will know it and we will be filled with unmatched joy.

There will be no more tiny glimpses. The connection will not fade as it does now, causing

> Notice what happens to our spirit when all is right in our relationship with God.

us to return to the scriptures, fellowship and prayer to renew our spirit. We are united with the Spirit of God even now if we are able to see past the tests and trials, and by faith accept the free gift of salvation. Then we can become true friends of God on our journey in knowing Him.

> Once we are in God's presence, life will finally be complete. Our hearts and spirits will know it and we will be filled with unmatched joy.

The Scripture was fulfilled which says, "Abraham believed God, and it was reckoned to Him as righteousness," and he was called the friend of God (James 2: 23).

God created us in His image so that we can be a reflection of Him and His kingdom in a fantastic variety of ways. What a challenge God had in mind for His children—to hope in an unseen place! Heaven is our Father's house; a place of eternal joy and fellowship, not just with God, but with each other. That fellowship is the reflection of the fel-

> When our hearts are touched, life seems to be complete in some sort of way.

lowship God the Father has enjoyed with the Son and the Holy Spirit and He wants us to experience that joy too. Death is just the doorway to the realm of heaven. In Philippians 3: 20 we are told that our citizenship is not here, but with God in heaven. We are only visitors here waiting to go home. The evil one will have no power there—this is truly good news!

> Heaven is in a completely different dimension and we are called to reside there.

Unhindered Joy

Have you ever watched a little child clap in delight they accomplish something? They are filled with open, honest, unbridled joy! There is no pretention nor guile, just pure happiness. They receive gifts the same way. God desires that we come to Him like a child and receive His gift of Christ and eternal life with the same kind of happy authenticity!

When children feel loved, safe, and cared for, they can securely explore their world. We enjoy watching them experience life to the fullest, with the freedom to be themselves, unencumbered by constraints of any sort. They have no fear that family or friends will criticize or reject them; societal boundaries have not yet hemmed them in. A spiritually healthy child may not even know the meaning of the word fear. They are thrilled to experience life and simply live in the moment.

> God wants to communicate an extraordinary plan that was specifically designed for every single one of His extraordinary people.

> A child is born with an innate desire to be loved.

There is immense joy in experiencing God's presence. In the book of Proverbs, Solomon was filled with a spirit of awestruck delight when he walked with the Lord:

> *Then I was beside Him, as a master workman; and I was daily His delight, Rejoicing always before Him, Rejoicing in the world, His earth, and having my delight in the sons of men*

> Proverbs 8: 30–31

Passion in Action

God's passion has an intensity that is not easily understood. God expresses Himself in ways that appear to go on forever, just as His love for us does. His love has a depth, breadth and scope beyond our imagination.

When we approach the Lord in authentic faith; with honesty and humility, God rejoices. Just as the father of the prodigal son rejoiced in his son's return, so our Heavenly Father rejoices when we come to Him. God continually shows man His love and mercy through the created world. Think about a sunbeam piercing the clouds to illuminate a mountain ridge, a rainbow appearing in the mist of a thundering waterfall or the night darkness being broken by the flashing of fireflies—these are loving expressions of God's creation. The Lord put these elements in place to communicate His delight in His creation and to show us through this gift, His love and passion towards us!

All of this was designed and ordered before the very beginning. It is a challenge for us in our needy, distracted, fleshy state to imagine a time before creation. God gives us an idea of what it was like when He speaks to Job out of a storm. God's powerful speech to Job speaks to all of us and reminds us of God's unmatched power and intelligence.

> God has an intensity of passion not easily understood by man.

Let's put ourselves in Job's place for a minute and listen to what God is saying to him through the storm:

"Brace yourself like a man. I will question you and you shall answer me." Picture this scene: The Lord is speaking to Job out of a storm. This is not a typical rain shower. The Bible doesn't use fancy print or interactive graphics to make a point. We have to take it for what it says—out of a storm. A storm ordered by God Himself! This is the real moment in time—a "life drama" unfolding before our eyes. With thunder, real thunder, in his voice, God asks Job, "Where were you when I laid the earth's foundations? Tell me if you understand"! In our minds, we hear the horrible peels of thunder and see the white—hot veins of lightening flash across the sky, like a divine exclamation point as God speaks. He continues, "Who marked off its dimensions? Surely you know"! FLASH! CRACK! "Who stretched a measuring line across it? On what were its footings set, or who laid its cornerstone"? (Job 38: 3 to Job 42: 5)

God had warned Job to brace himself for this questioning, and rightfully so! The impact of the moment was a multi-sensory experience, perhaps overloading all of Job's senses! God's words and nature were firing simultaneously! God doesn't speak out of storms often; God is bringing attention to this point in scripture for a reason.

> The Bible doesn't use fancy print or interactive graphics to make a point.

God is challenging Job and making statements about His glorious creations. Part of the list includes: the morning stars, angels, the springs of the sea, clouds, gates-of-death, gates-of-the-shadow-of-death, the abode-of-light, darkness, snow, hail, east winds, rain, storm-fronts, ice, frost, the constellations Pleiades and Orion, bears and bear cubs, laws of the heavens and lightning bolt destinations—and God is just getting started! He continues with eagles, horses, and even behemoths. Chapters 38 through 41 are worth careful reading, just to let all of this imagery soak in.

What is the purpose of this list of powerful, and often terrifying images of nature? Job had lost perspective during his trial. Why else would God have questioned him? God was trumping Job to make him think, to restore his perspective as a God-fearing, God-trusting, and God-loving man.

God may not speak to us directly out of storms today, but He speaks to us through many other life-storms and trials. The 5th chapter of Matthew states that it "rains on the just and unjust." In the book of

> Job had lost perspective in his trial. God was trumping Job to make him think; to restore his perspective.

James, we find the words, "when you encounter various trials . . ." (notice that it says when, not if). When we study the literary devices in the Bible, we decipher basic biblical concepts integral to understanding who God is.

In Job's trial, God points

to the original design and elements of His creations as testimony to His profound sovereignty and supremacy. He is not to be questioned.

God is pointing with a purpose, "Have you comprehended the vast expanses of the earth"? There's a reason He asked this. He wants us to meditate on His great wonders. Trying to comprehend the complexities of this world and the vast expanses of the galaxies will help us engage with God as Creator; opening our hearts, restoring us and giving us a new perspective.

> Job says that he now "sees." He is finally seeing with the eyes of his heart! I believe Job is also seeing with the eyes of his soul for the first time.

If we can look beyond the crisis of the moment, the tyranny of the urgent, the distractions of the enemy, if we can turn off the TV, unplug from are digital devices or quit texting our friends for a while, God has an awesome message for us. When we recognize that there is something bigger than us in the moment; that is a great beginning. The core of Job's being got the message.

> *I have heard of You by the hearing of the ear;*
> *But now my eye sees You;*
>
> Job 42: 5

Job says that he now "sees." He is finally seeing with the eyes of his heart. I believe Job is also seeing with the eyes of His soul for the first time. Surely an awakening and a renewal of his perspective took place.

Perspective

When we lose perspective on the bigness of God, we are in pretty serious trouble. We begin to murmur and complain. We become hopeless and despondent. This loss of sight can put our thoughts into a death spiral. In other words, we loose our significant connection with God.

We are without our spiritual compass.

We may not know that our perspective is skewed and just continue on our path, headed for dark days. There is sadness and a lack of joy in losing sight of God and who we are in Him. We may chalk it up to the school of hard knocks. We may think life is miserable and we need to learn to live with it. As we spiral further down, life situations can get worse, compounding upon one another like freight cars in a train wreck. Unfortunately our relationships with others become affected and we isolate ourselves and push others away. The enemy loves to help us down any destructive path. Rather than handing us tissues and consoling us with uplifting words, he rocks back and forth on his heels with an evil grin, pleased with our heartbreak, and watches as we experience mental and spiritual bankruptcy.

> Understanding God's passion means that we truly *experience* it.

We may have a wonderful family, a successful business, a secure job packed with promotions, but we can still sometimes focus on the negative, that which we don't have. The tremendous amount of discouragement can be overwhelming, so the leap from a spiritual death to a physical one may seem easy to make. Then the enemy is overjoyed.

Some believe they should bury themselves in doing good; to singing in the choir, working on the hostess team, serving as an usher or taking meals to shut-ins. They believe these things will make them whole again. These are all

> When we lose perspective on the bigness of God, we are in pretty serious trouble.

worthy pursuits; however, good works alone will not get to the heart of the issue. God's Word tells us that even the religious leaders can get

> The enemy loves to help us along down any destructive path.

caught in the good works trap. Jesus tells His followers in Matthew 7: 22–23 that many will say that they prophesied and cast out demons and performed many miracles in my name, but in the end I will tell them go away because I never knew you. Jesus is defining (for the entire world), those who know Him and those who don't. This clear distinction, which exhorts believers to know God (not just know of Him, but actually have a relationship with Him), prompts us to start checking the condition of our hearts.

In this pursuit, we run the risk of being blind-sided. The enemy is very good at this. We may tell ourselves, "All my needs are met and all that I am doing is successful, so what do I need God for"? This seems to be a current trend in our materialistic world, but God desires for us to keep Him in the center of our perspective at all times.

We must seek only that which is God's wise plan for our lives. If the kingdom of God is not sought, it will not be found. Even King Solomon, the wisest man on earth, lost his heavenly perspective when he had

> This clear distinction, which exhorts believers to know God (not just know of Him, but actually have a *relationship* with Him), prompts us to start checking the condition of our hearts.

everything His heart desired—everything that worldly success and fame could bring. If it happened to him, it can easily happen to us. Proverbs 30: 7–9 reads, "Two things I ask of you, O LORD; do not refuse me before I die: Keep falsehood and lies far from me, give me neither poverty nor riches, but give me only my daily bread. Otherwise, I may have too much and disown you and say, 'Who is the LORD?' Or I may become poor and steal and so dishonor the name of my God."

Keeping a simple, healthy, God-inclusive perspective is of great significance. Engaging with God's Word and remembering the deeds He has lovingly and passionately done for us will help us keep a right-minded perspective and a God-centered heart:

I shall remember the deeds of the Lord; Surely I will remember
Your wonders of old. I will meditate on all Your work and muse
on Your deeds. Your way, O God, is holy; What god is great like
our God? You are the God who works wonders; You have made
known Your strength among the peoples.

Psalm 77: 11–14

What is God's inspiration for creation? We are!

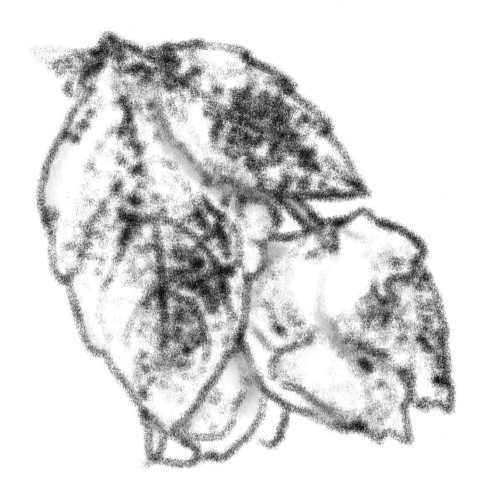

4
God's Creation: Get the Message

When we visit new places, like the local zoo, aquarium, or local park, we can miss the handiwork of God if we are not looking for it. This chapter will provide keys to catch God's vision in creation. If you see God's vision, you have experienced an epiphany—a peek into heaven!

James 3: 17 states, "But the wisdom that is from above is first pure, then peaceful, gentle, reasonable, full of mercy and good fruits, without partiality, and without hypocrisy." The next time you experience wisdom from above, recognize the influence it has on you physically. When you hear truth that touches your core, you take a breath. This isn't the usual shallow breathing we are accustomed too, but a full, involuntary deep breath. It's almost impossible to avoid doing it!

> If you can catch God's vision, you have experienced an epiphany—a peek into heaven!

This breath is a shot of wisdom from above and it comes with a side serving of peace. When information conflicts with a truth that resides in our hearts, or when someone touches on a personal area that needs addressing, we may swallow hard or our palms may sweat.

The next time you feel that you are reacting physically to news or a particular event, ask yourself, "What is God trying to tell me through simple bodily functions?" Whether it's a facial blush, or that sick feeling in the pit of your stomach, or becoming weak-kneed—take a moment to engage your mind and process what is happening on a physical level. Try to think about things on a cause and effect basis. These effects are not knee-jerk reactions or animal instincts. These emotions are connected to our hearts and our passions. They're found in the intimate details of our orig-

> When you hear truth that touches your very core, your body wants to take a breath.

inal design and discovered by us as we engage with our Creator God. When was the last time that you saw a monkey blush?

Those of us with children have great opportunities to demonstrate how loving, friendly and creative God is. Teaching children about the design process can give them a sense of wonder, and help bring a perceived distant God much closer. Close enough to see that He loves all of us dearly.

Adults can personally enjoy God's creations based on their unique experiences, educational backgrounds and insights from the Holy Spirit.

We're drawn to our occupations for different reasons. From an engineer's perspective, the wonder of creation is in its structure and methodology. Most engineers are master problem solvers and have a drive to grasp the mysteries of how things work. They have a desire to solve structural problems, and because of their gifts and talents, engineers have a natural curiosity toward the inner workings of things. We're not all wired like engineers, but engineers, responding to their God-designed perspective, will see the creative mind of God in their own ways as they explore creation.

A nurse, with the gift of mercy, may see God's loving heart by exploring creations that bring comfort to those who are hurting (something that seems second nature to most nurses). For example, a nurse may enjoy growing flowers, and he or she may realize the comfort these can bring to people. Giving flowers is an act of kindness, which is so good for those who need to know others care. The scent of a rose, the color of the carnation and beauty of a calla lily can all remind us that life is bigger than what we define merely in earthly terms.

When was the last time that you saw a monkey blush?

An artist may be attracted to creations that are colorful, playful or offer an intriguing shape or pattern. Translucency or texture on the underside of a leaf may be a point of inspiration. Visuals that express depth through perspective—a tree line, or railroad tracks that disappear in the distance—can appeal to the creative soul. Repetition in shape, design, asymmetry or perfect symmetry may be found in a flowering vine or in an unusual rock formation where colors seem to dance together. Pleasing composition may be found in the radiance of "sweet light"[1] or in the reflection on a lake's surface or on an ocean's wave .

I asked a friend, Andy Sparks, what aspect of his occupation as a landscape architect wows him (I call this the "awe factor.")? He handed me one of the magazine articles he wrote for an association he belonged to. The excerpt reads,

". . . A little two-acre woods and field by my house has something in bloom from March until November and fruit and seed for much longer. What kink in evolution or natural selection caused some trees and shrubs to develop so they would bloom on woody tissue in February or March, others on woody tissue in April or May or June, others on new growth in May, June, July or August, and still others on woody tissue in July, August, September, October, or November? Why do daisies and ragweed grow where asters, raspberries and strawberries grow? Why is there something always in bloom, in fruit, or in seed everywhere you look almost all year long? Luck? No, because another part of creation is there to use it. Nothing is wasted."

Another excerpt from Andy, titled "Symmetry by Chance or Design?" reveals a similar rejection of macroevolution ideology:

"While looking in an old photo album a while back, I noticed that across several generations of several unrelated families, we were all pretty much symmetrically constructed—two arms, two eyes, two legs, five fingers and toes on each hand and foot. . . Then I was at the zoo checking out our furry and feathered friends in the lower orders of the animal kingdom and I noticed the same thing about them. Legs, ears, eyes, nostrils, fins, gills, etc., all symmetrically arranged!. . . Last weekend I was watching a handful of beneficial insects take aim at the billions of foliage eaters in my yard. Oddly enough, all those bugs, worms, moths, insects, spiders, aphids, ants, wasps, beetles, etc., had symmetry. Even the leaves that were being eaten were symmetrical, and the flowers and the seed pods and fruits . . ."

The symmetry in two eyes gives us depth perception and substantially increases our peripheral vision. Participation in sports, driving, and everything else we do is much easier with two eyes! Someone once said that one eye is the backup to the other. The eye is one of the most vulnerable parts of our exposed bodies. . . so God gave us a spare!

Symmetry goes deep! We even have brains that are right and left sided! One of Andy's gifts for engaging with God's creation is the deep appreciation and wonder he has for things made by God. Andy continues to question the evolution of the human species by asking the following:

> "What makes our physical eyes possible without a concept of vision?. . . That takes a lot more than brain or eyes. It takes a certain light and atmosphere. And, why would an eye evolve? How could the force behind evolution have any foreknowledge about vision and if the conditions were right to permit it?"
>
> Andy Sparks,
> Landscape Architect

Many people are not aware of the God-given spiritual gifts they have. We can easily get distracted from using them. Get in touch with your spiritual gifts. You'll find a tool or two for perceiving God's creations by engaging your gifts. There are questionnaires available designed to reveal your spiritual gifts.

Considering Creation

God tells us to "consider the lilies" He wants us to meditate upon all of His marvelous deeds! But what did He mean by the word "consider"? Webster aids us in defining this important word:

> **Consider:** To think about carefully; to think of especially with regard to taking some action, to take into account / to regard or treat in an attentive or kindly way / to gaze on steadily or reflectively / to come to judge or classify / to regard / to suppose / to reflect / to deliberate.

We are encouraged to consider the Bible; not merely perform a cursory reading of the stories that were so carefully written on these pages, but to *savor* the words of the Bible and keep them in our hearts. It may take some effort to slow down and think deeply about this life instruction manual God wrote through the power of the Holy Spirit. You will find it well worth it! The messages may be a whisper, at first, but as we fine tune our listening skills, and spend more time with Him, the message will become clearer. This requires patience and prayers. We must see with new perspective. We may get frustrated if we don't feel like God is responding to us right away. Many of us would prefer for God to just write the answer in the sky if we should marry that special someone. We wish He would send us an email with detailed instructions if we should take that job offer, or which university our child should attend. But He requires much more from us, and it starts with learning all we can about our Designer.

What was the specific purpose of creation?

As a help in making general creation observations as to what went into the creative process, one important question to ask ourselves is "What is/was (if extinct), the specific purpose of a particular creation"?

I use a H.E.A.V.E.N. acronym to help spot God's *Before the Beginning* design:

Humor:	Funny bone = healing bone
Extremes:	Longest, shortest, fastest, slowest, hottest, coldest, hairiest, loudest, lightest, heaviest, weakest, strongest, thinnest, thickest, etc.
Awe Factor:	It should be *jaw* factor: How far does your jaw drop?
Variety:	Who doesn't like variety?
Everyone:	Did the designer have you and me in mind?
Nuts and Bolts Practicality:	Things that hold things together or are necessary for living, or functioning

Humor

God has a sense of humor. He invented it! Just look at the faces of monkeys and some dogs. There are pug dogs that look like they tried walking through a glass door. There are animals of every sort with silly features and abilities. God wants to crack us up! Proverbs states "laughter is healing to the bones." And we want bones to be in their best condition, they are the structure that holds us up! Without bones, we could do nothing! Bones are also the foundation of our unique identities. The bones provide rigidity to protect us from most of life's bumps and bruises. Bones are where the muscles are secured. Our bones create white blood cells so we can fight infection. Along with muscles, tendons, ligaments, organs, etc., the bones give us support for our mobility.

> God has a sense of humor. He invented it!

If creation makes us laugh, we may be experiencing creation just the way God intended. There is a reason for every living creature on the earth, no matter how odd they might seem.

One of the most unusual, but common animals is the skunk. Why would God want to make on oversized striped rodent that is armed with a portable bio-chemical attack manufacturing facility? Can God smell the pungent odor when a skunk gets cornered and responds with

Monkey Face Orchid (really—just search it on-line!)

a stench-packed stream? The smell can travel for miles. It lingers for days, and it seems to permeate everything! When dogs get sprayed, we douse them in a mix of Hydrogen Peroxide, dish soap and baking soda. So what good is this foul-smelling beast?

> Yes, even the skunk has a reason for existence.

Even the skunk has a reason for existence. Maybe it's to remind us that really stinky stuff sometimes happens. Keep away from stinky stuff. . . perhaps it's an analogy to sin, or maybe it's just to make us laugh when we see one another's faces scrunched up in smell defense mode! Whatever the reason, when the skunk lifts its tail, it has our complete and unwavering attention!

The nose is able to distinguish ten thousand different smells.[2] Referred to by many as the schnoz, the sniffer, the whiffer, smeller, honker, schnozola and sneezer, the genius is in the placement of this appendage. We can be thankful it's at the helm of our bodies. God even made the nose capable of losing a smell in a matter of seconds if we must spend long periods near tainted odors. Mercy and kindness were demonstrated by this thoughtful design feature *before* the beginning! Creation is filled with humor!

What about the frog fish? This fish comes complete with its own, baited fishing pole! This is how the fish hunts. A pole comes out of his head while a smaller fish goes for the bait. The frog fish then snaps up the fooled fish with his frog-like tongue! Plenty of human fishermen and women wish they had the luck of a frog fish when they cast their bait.

My family and I took a visit to the Cincinnati Aquarium where we saw an animal called a pyjama shark. It literally looks like it is wearing pajamas and dances about half out of the water! It also swims towards visitors and shoots water at their faces. At another

> Creation is filled with humor!

Cincinnati park, there was a plaque at the location where a skeleton of a bear-size beaver was found. It had buckteeth the size of the blade of a garden hoe! Can you imagine coming face to face with one of those?

We need to take the time to experience creation the way God wants us to see things. Look with a creative eye! Look for the humor! God put these things here for our pleasure! We take pleasure in seeing our kids enjoy each other, toys, critters and creation. I believe that God experiences a similar joy seeing us delight in discovering His creations.

> God was play-
> ful in His design.
> Just look at the
> porcupine, the
> platypus and the
> pink flamingo!

God was playful in His design. Just look at the porcupine, the platypus and the pink flamingo! This playfulness is what the enemy wants to conceal from us. As we remove the enemy's blinders via prayer, we will be able to see the joy, humor and playful attributes of our Creator.

God's love transcends the constraints of this earthy place. Paul states in Corinthians that, "No eye has seen, no ear has heard, no mind has conceived what God has prepared for those who love Him." In addition to what God has put on earth, He is preparing something beyond what we can conceive. God allowed some of His works to be experienced here on earth, prior to His works in heaven. John 14: 3 tells us Jesus is preparing a place for us. Seeing God's transcendent playfulness in His Design, we catch a glimpse of things to come. That same good-humored spirit is often reflected in our own nature. God's lightheartedness shines to glorify Himself! Here are a few other creations that exhibit playfulness in design:

- A flying fish, an oxymoron in itself!
- The octopus and jellyfish flash an array of brilliant colors.
- Our feathered friends can come with outlandish headdresses, slipper-like feathered feet and feather designs so unique that they have been used in paintings, fabrics and Tiffany

lamps for centuries.

- The penguin, pelican and puffer fish all have distinctive shapes exaggerated or out-of-place features.

> Seeing God's transcendent playfulness in His Design, we catch a glimpse of things to come.

- The night's soothing sounds are like a divine lullaby. The spring peeper's rhythmic sounds, the ribbits and bellows of the toad, and the steady chirps of crickets sooth the soul for a good night's rest. And it's fun to mimic the deep twang of the bullfrog with rubber bands!
- A songbird's cheery melody and a rooster's crow are great sounds to start a day!
- Polly the parrot does want a cracker! This bird was designed to mimic our speech!
- A stick that walks! Tree leafs that fly! Finding an incognito walking stick insect or a Dry Leaf Butterfly are delightful surprises.
- Spots and stripes are all over tigers, giraffes and zebras. Maybe God is working on a checkered cheetah or a heavenly animal that sports a primitive plaid! Because we can't conceive God's creative work in our current finite thoughts, what He has in heaven for us might be really different!

> The night's soothing sounds are like a divine lullaby.

And what about the act of play itself? Carefree fun is enjoyed by young, uncluttered souls, more than by complicated, distracted adults. The "purity of spirit" exhibited when a child skips from room to room or glides through the air on a swing is often lost by older generations. And as we stand at the window, with our briefcase or laundry basket in one hand and a bag of groceries in the other, we realize that something has changed within us. We wonder what happened to our carefree selves. We all have responsibilities so on weekends or holidays, we try to make time for relaxation and fun. How do we maintain a playful *spirit*? It's not so much the activity, but the carefree state of a child's mind which fills our backyards and playgrounds with giggles and belly laughs.

When God tells us to come to Him like a child, He encourages us to approach Him with simple intentions and honest faith. Jesus says to draw near to Him and He will draw near to us. Jesus asks for the pure innocence of children when He tells us to come to Him as a child. In a soothing, Father-like tone, God tells us, "I know who you were meant to be. I understand who you really are. I made you. I knew you when you were being formed in your mother's womb. I love you child. I have come to give you a full life, a hope and a future. I want to hold you in my arms. I want you under my wings as a hen secures her chicks. I died for you, so every ounce of guilt and shame, all feelings of rejection and self condemnation can be put away for eternity."

God desires for our spirits to be just as He created them: free and unencumbered by any worldly entanglements, dancing joyously, fully celebrating the intended purity of mind, spirit and being.

> Carefree fun is enjoyed by young uncluttered souls more than by complicated, distracted adults.

For you were called to freedom, brethren; only do not turn your freedom into an opportunity for the flesh, but through love serve one another.

Galatians 5: 13

> It's not so much the activity, but the carefree state of a child's mind which fills our backyards and playgrounds with giggles and belly laughs.

A keen sense of humor helps us to overlook the unbecoming, understand the unconventional, tolerate the unpleasant, overcome the unexpected, and outlast the unbearable.

Billy Graham, Evangelist

Every ounce of guilt and shame, all feelings of rejection and self condemnation can be put away for eternity.

Extremes

There is a message to us in the extremes found in nature. The butterfly is one of the king of extremes. In its extreme molecular metamorphosis, it changes from one form to another. A caterpillar makes itself into a chrysalis, in minutes; complete with reflective gold trimmings!

Butterflies emerging from their chrysalis, have been compared to Christ rising from the tomb. Their extreme beauty and unbelievable engineering is something to behold. One butterfly, the North American Monarch, has the unique ability to fly as far as 3,000 miles each year to the same precise location!

Let's focus upon two specific creatures living in extremes. The first is the deep-sea, volcano-dwelling, blind shrimp. The other is the ice worm. The blind shrimp resides at the mouth of volcanoes in water temperatures measuring 700° F. Poisonous hydrogen sulfide and methane come out of these vents.[3] Stop and think about this enigma. These heat-resistant shrimp exist in colonies, deep in the ocean, under tons of pressure. Most meats like chicken, beef, pork and fish become safe to eat at 160° F. Many metals become molten when exposed to 700° F heat. Welders set their torches to this temperature to cut metal. How can this tiny, tough crustacean survive in this extreme heat?

Scientists need to search for answers. They have the tenacity, and focus to find measurable clues. These answers must be acceptable to

Ten-minute transformation from caterpillar to chrysalis.

the scientific community. What happens when the piece doesn't fit the puzzle, like the enigmatic volcano shrimp? This delicacy should be served on a bed of rice with sweet teriyaki sauce on the side! It defies physics, plain and simple. (Still, scientists continue in their quest, never ceasing to seek the answer.)

God has wired us with a void that only He can fill. If we try to fill it with something else, we are fully deceived. God cannot be put in a box and He likes it that way. How blessed we are to have our God! His non-conforming, physics-busting trump cards keep life fresh and mysterious! These extremes keep us looking to the original Designer in awe.

We also find extreme creatures creeping along at the other end of the temperature scale.

> There is a message for us in the extremes found in nature.

Can anything thrive in solid ice? Yes! It's our Freon-filled friend the ice worm.[4] According to scientists, there is a three-inch worm that makes its way through glaciers. We understand earthworms aerating soil. But why do we need our glaciers aerated? Maybe the ice worm creates breaking points for transformation.

Furthermore, how does this worm eat, live and even reproduce. . . all while contained in a alabaster berg? And why? Can we learn something from nature's frigid and rigid breaking point? Maybe God made it just because He can. Perhaps He wanted to confound us and point us to Him.

As we think about more extremes in creation, we come across the colossal dinosaurs. At the *Answers In Genesis Biblical Creation Museum* in Kentucky, there is a dinosaur exhibit that is fully loaded with animatronics. Hollywood, at its best, couldn't beat the quality of these high-tech beasts. They roar, snort and one of them even reaches down to take a bite out the next curious visitor! Perhaps it's good that these extremely monstrous creatures are extinct. Life has enough trouble, without one

> God has wired us with a void that only He can fill. If we try to fill it with something else, we are fully deceived.

of these giants roaming our park trails on a bright spring day! The museum also has a planetarium with a rare presentation of the extreme size and precise order of the universe. A visit to the Creation Museum is well worth the trip. And don't forget to check out the Ark Encounter. A full scale, walk through ark will give you a sense of awe and wonder on the inspired work of Noah and his sons.

Awe Factor

Could experiencing awe be what it's all about? God created and we experience it. It touches our hearts and *we see God's order of life!* We smile warmly inside and get a sense of our Creator's handiwork. When this happens, our heart opens up a bit more. As a result, we may attend church or synagogue for the first time. We may have shed our first tear in years. Or, we may just end up in a contemplative state of awesome wonder.

> God cannot be put in a box and He likes it that way.

The Awe Factor can happen upon observation of any part of God's creation. It involves our senses. We may hear, touch or feel something that was inspired by God. It strikes a chord within our souls. For just a moment, we sense the enormous force it took to create it and our view of life gets strangely bigger. We pause for a moment and we instinctively feel and express. . . Awe.

These moments happen in individual ways because we are created to be unique. What causes the Awe Factor in one person may not be the same in another. We must be open to them and watch for these moments. Experiences like these help us grow closer to whom we were meant to be when God first began to form us.

One of the most common ways to experience the Awe Factor is through music. Here in Ohio, a local harp instructor put on a harp ensemble every year just before Christmas. There are usually 12–15 harpists present. All ages are represented.

The harp symbolizes peace and tranquility. Artists of old have depicted cherubs fluttering about with harps in hand. Is the simplicity of life's beauty found in a plucked string? David played the harp for King Saul, who enjoyed the heavenly strings continually, because it comforted his tortured soul.

When the harp ensemble began playing, the sound resonated to my core. At the far end of the row, a little Asian girl, no more than eight years old, was playing a harp that was nearly as big as she was. At the opposite end of the row, an elderly woman played her instrument with just

> These moments happen to us in individual ways because we were created uniquely.

as much enthusiasm as the seven year old. They were both putting their hearts into the music and it was easy to see their passion.

The magical notes of harmonies rushed toward me and. . . Wham! My eyes began to puddle with emotion. I was caught up in the moment. This musical journey touched my soul in immeasurable ways. Joy and contentment seem to ease my heart as it was certainly a stressful time in our lives. I breathed deeply and my soul settled.

What went on here? I am not completely sure. Was it a rush of understanding of things required to make the evening a success? Several different styles of harps, such as the Classical and Celtic were played. Was it an acknowledgement of the man-hours and care it took to make each harp? Maybe it was the timbre each harp produced or the beautiful sound of all of them playing, simultaneously. Was it the instructor's years of experience, the focus, the passion to keep doing what she believed in? Or the hours of practice and lessons or was it a specific song being played? Was it a combination of things? There is no doubt in my mind that something beyond this world took place as I experienced

> Perhaps one of the most common ways to experience the Awe Factor is through music.

this moment, and it was wonderful and pleasantly overwhelming! Analyzing the experience wasn't important or needed during the concert—I was just simply touched and filled with, a God or Spirit-given awe.

The Awe-Inspiring Universe

Our universe is skillfully described in a book entitled *Taking Back Astronomy, The Heavens Declare Creation*, by Dr. Jason Lisle, astrophysicist. Dr. Lisle makes some observations that prompt grand wonder. For example, to help understand the distance between the earth and the sun, Lisle estimates that it would take a person traveling at 65 mph, 163 years to reach the sun. That distance is just the right amount so we don't burn or freeze. Are all of these amazing celestial arrangements merely accidents? A drive to Pluto would take 6,500 years at 65 mph![5] Were these starry night-lights put into place just to steer our ships or is there deeper meaning to be discovered?

> ### Are all of these amazing celestial arrangements merely accidents?

Dr. Lisle brilliantly illuminates the sizes of the sun and the moon visible diameters are spatially the same (angular size).[6] The moon and the sun's diameters from earth happen to be the diameter of a common writing instrument. If both were depicted in a painting or photograph, they would measure about a ¼" in diameter. Can you believe that something so spatially insignificant in our view is able to give us enough light to see, grow our crops, warm the waters and assist so greatly in sustaining life as we know it? If the sun had an angular size of a 9.5" basketball we would have like-size blind spots from an inadvertent glance. A few of these incidents with our current eye structure would likely cause permanent blindness.

Can you imagine the design challenges that faced God as He sat behind His drawing board of life? Hypothetically, was God scratching His giant head and thinking out loud? What would He be saying to Himself? Maybe it went something like this:

"OK, I need a life-and-light-giving source—let's call it the sun—and we'll use hydrogen as its fuel. It should perpetually burn to create heat and light that should radiate the right living conditions about 94 million miles from the earth. . . No, on second thought, that is a little too far away and my creations might get a little too chilly. 92 million miles away would be devastatingly too hot, so let's put it at 93 million miles away; that should be just about perfect. If they choose, my creations can move a little bit south to feel more warmth from the sun. I hope they can feel my love for them in my careful creation of the sun and the placement of all the planets, moons and all of the stars in the sky. I have created all of this. . . for them."

Imagining God's careful loving thoughts created again, in me, the Awe Factor!

Variety

Most of us like variety. Because of this, we can purchase miniature shrink-wrapped cereal boxes, 31 flavors of ice cream at Baskin Robbins®7 and hundreds of channels in our cable packages! We enjoy diversity! To quote a popular motto: "Variety is the spice of life!"

God created variety in everything! As Paul Garner shares in his book, *The New Creationism*, we have about "1.7 million species of plants, animals, fungi, microbes and other forms of life that have been identified and named by biologists, but estimates of the total number of species on Earth vary greatly from ten million to 100 million."8

Pick your favorite creation and think about it for a minute. Let's take flowers for example. The variety and transitional colors of floral species are extraordinary. Color in and of itself gives us pep and excitement, especially on a dreary day. Color on a flower decorates our fields, our homes and our walkways. Attach a flower to almost anything, and it will cheer up the space! Give flowers to someone who has done something nice for you, or give a flowering plant

> Can you imagine the design challenges that faced God as He sat behind His drawing board of life?

to anyone and it will brighten their day!

Isn't it marvelous that God made our brains flower-reactive? Neuroscience says when we see something that evokes pleasure, our brains produce endorphins (happy chemicals that permeate other areas of our brain besides optic and visual centers). The sight and scent of a flower can make us feel very good, if not loved. When they are picked they just need a little water. They're lightweight, so we can take them anywhere. The softness of a petal is unlike any other natural texture. The variety of colors, scents, sizes, textures and functions that flowers come in is staggering. In fact, one variety of lily offers pollen that attracts only one bee on only one day of the year, the melipona bee. Only this particular bee knows the secret to pollinating this awesome plant and without it, we would have no vanilla bean![9] Thank the Creator that this happens, or we would certainly have to survive with fewer varieties of cakes, cookies, pies and other desserts, for *we would have no vanilla today* or any other day.

> Isn't it marvelous that God made our brains flower-reactive?

> The Great Creator provides us with an abundance of visual complexity in His work.

Our brain is designed to highly welcome variety. Our miraculous nose, the wiring to the brain from the nose, and the brain itself can in a brief sniff, interpret the difference between the scent of a rose and the scent of a carnation! If flowers aren't your thing then the smell of a 12 oz. steak sizzling on a grill will do the trick. We are wired to be "reactive" to different things!

The Great Creator provides us with an abundance of visual complexity in His work. On the following page is a print representing the variety found in a small specie-sampling of our feathered friends. The

Too many !! in this book

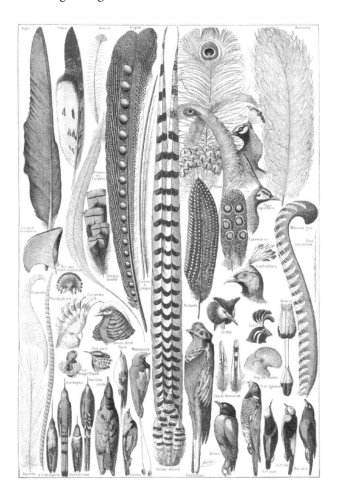

Plumes

detail, design, construction and functionality observed in a simple quill, can leave one speechless.

Butterflies come in various colors, shapes, sizes and a wide assortment of species. The Owl Butterfly is so named because the patterns on its wings resemble the eyes of an owl. The white-feathered stippling on the tip of the butterfly's wings makes the entire body of the butterfly look like an owl's head. We understand this coloring is for camouflage, a defense mechanism to scare away predators. If you look at the wings from the Awe Factor, it becomes an artist's canvas. We then see the Designer's skill; pure brilliance. There are well-conceived patterns, balance and pure symmetry of design. Elements of color, texture and shape create interest and intrigue the observer.

Look further and discover divine workmanship. There is a 3-D quality to the pattern and colors. Warm and cool colors make depth visible and pleasing. The fine markings, as if painted with a small sable-paintbrush, illustrate form. Fine color gradients, like strokes of a paintbrush, create the illusions of highlight and shadow. Each stroke helps to show form and the glassy imitation "eyes." Even the depths of eye sockets are depicted! The wing's canvas-like surface is not overworked as a beginning artist might do. This butterfly masterpiece reflects a relaxed artist enjoying himself, who knew exactly what He wanted to accomplish.

Owl Butterfly

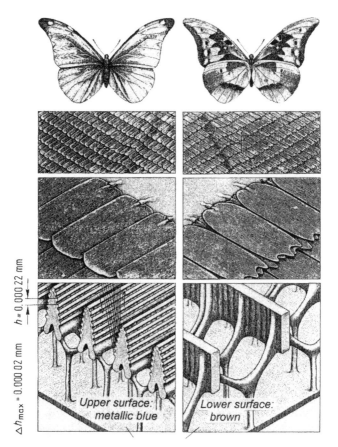

$h = 0.000\,22$ mm

$\Delta h_{max} = 0.000\,02$ mm

Upper surface: metallic blue

Lower surface: brown

Morpho Rhetenor Butterfly
Magnification: 20,000 times[10]

God designed the Owl Butterfly to frighten away its predators. But I believe He also designed this handiwork to be appreciated by His people from continent to continent as it migrates its flight! Its intricacy and beauty are not to be viewed on a gallery wall. This amazing painting is on the six-inch winged-canvas of what some may consider an insignificant creature—a butterfly!

> God created the colors found on the Blue Morpho butterfly without pigments!

The above picture is the South American Blue Morpho Rhetenor butterfly with wing surface sections under different magnifications. God created the colors found on the Blue Morpho Rhetenor butterfly without pigments! It looks so vivid, as if someone had dipped its wings in cans of bright electric blue paint. God used light refraction and light deletion to create color!

Wow! (Are you beginning to experience the Awe Factor yet?) All that intricate preparation for a few weeks of flight! Just a few weeks earlier this butterfly was a translucent ooze transforming from a caterpillar to its new state. Why all this fuss? Assume for a moment that each one of these is an artist's canvas. These artworks, in their splendidly vast variety, get great exposure, although the work is unsigned. Maybe we are to acknowledge the artist's identity on faith and offer our uninhibited applause. This is what faithful followers call praise.

> Are you beginning to experience an Awe Factor yet?

The magnification of butterfly wings also demonstrates order and intention of design. What keeps this tiny creature suspended in flight? And what would we see at 200,000 times magnification? Just as perception of eternity can reach past the celestial, also perception of eternity can be found in very tiny things. It goes on forever!. . . It's all designed and managed, whether it's creatures on land, in the sea or in the air.

> Just as perception of eternity can reach past the celestial, also perception of eternity can be found in very, very tiny things. It goes on forever!

Form, function, beauty and wonder can be found everywhere, all intended for you and for me. God did not want us to become aloof from His creation. King Solomon's rant in Ecclesiastes pointed out the vanity or meaninglessness of creation and our toils. When Solomon stated: "All has been named," gives us a clue that this indeed was a rant. Albeit, a wise man's rant. The big question here is if creation reveals God then how can it be meaningless? Hence, again, a rant from a man with an Adamic nature, in which he realizes nothing but God can fulfill us. Eventually, Solomon was able to summarize life objectively when He said, "Fear God and obey His commandments." This is one of scriptures most intuitive mandates. In Ecclesiastes 12:1, Solomon reminds us to "Remember your creator in the days of your youth, before the days of trouble come and the years approach when you will say, I find no pleasure in them." As kids we would whine, "Oh, I'm sooo bored!" Solomon offers another wise piece of advice: "Consider what God has done:..." Ecclesiastes 7: 13 Pages 84-86 expand on Solomon's story.

Everyone

All of creation is designed to grab our attention and make us think, to cause us to look to heaven and to help us to get the fact that God EXISTS! By immersing us in the vastness of God's creation, He has a motive in mind: love. God loves us and is passionately pursuing us. All that we see was put here to sustain life; your life and my life, and to demonstrate His abiding love.

God loves us and is passionately pursuing us.

God gives us time to make choices. Through good and bad decisions we pursue our dreams aggressively, to the best of our ability. If we chase our dreams to excess, it's easy to miss the messages given to us along the way. What's important to God should be important to us. After all, He did travel to the ends of the galaxy to name the stars and set all in perfect motion!

What else might God be asking?

"Will adults finally see themselves for who they are—my children? Will they be able to see themselves as a child that can't find the juice box. . . sitting front and center on the eye-level shelf of a refrigerator? Will they enter a state of utter-bewilderment because their own children can't see what is right in front of their faces"?

Perhaps God looks down, scratches His chin in wonder and says. . .

"I put my children right in the middle of my millions of creations, gave them an intellect and five highly sophisticated and extremely sensitive senses to explore these creations and you'd think they could see their Creator! It cracks me up every time someone finally gets it! Did I give them a little too much of my "know it all" attribute?"

> The first is to acknowledge God through a simple prayer—a prayer from your heart.

On the more serious note, some reject or rebel against God for various reasons. Some have gotten distracted because we are in an attention grabbing culture. Gamers and political news junkies both can easily get preoccupied. Some think it's not a convenient time to pursue the things of God. Many are finding themselves caught up in sexual addiction. Many sincerely believe they are following God, but are spending more time in front of the TV, on social media, or texting than they do learning about God and His Kingdom. God has shown, throughout history, that He is a very jealous God.

If you are not following God but would like to, may I suggest two things. The first is to acknowledge God through a simple prayer—a prayer from your heart. That's how we talk to Him. He tells us that He hears our prayers! The second is to contact a friend that is attending a Bible-based church and tell them of your interest. If you are unfamiliar

> God has shown throughout history that He is a very jealous God.

or new to the area, use a search engine to get connected with a local church. Use keywords related to some of your interests. E.g.: children's programs, men's study groups, divorce or grief recovery, teen programs, marriage enrichment, singles and/or senior gatherings, faith of interest, etc. You'll be pleasantly surprised on your findings as churches are trying to be relevant with their neighbors. Make it a point to visit the church and talk to a few people. Be patient, as finding a church can take a little time. Also keep in mind how you can use your gifts to help others. The sooner the concept of building *others* up is engaged, the more connected to things of God you'll be. Also, if want to take a backseat and listen to others interact for a long period, that can work as well. The point is to be hearing God's Word and to be meeting with His people. This is paramount in "seeking first His Kingdom." I am a huge fan of small bible study groups. These greatly help with Kingdom and heart building.

Getting to know God and His people can happen in so many ways—in a grocery line, a gas station, lumber yard or hair salon—virtually anywhere! Be sure to keep your God antenna pointing upwards, you'll be glad you did! Prayers have a way of making eternal connections.

> We are in a fallen world. Adam and Eve chose to disobey God. The effects of sin are everywhere.

Nuts and Bolts Practicality

It is remarkable how practical God is. How easy it is to take these creations for granted! We moan and groan about trivial issues, and get down when someone at church offends us. We can be absolute brats! Our family could be in great health, the kids doing great in school and we have a roof over our head, and still we are not counting our blessings and rejoicing continually. So what's our problem?

We are in a fallen world. Adam and Eve chose to disobey God. The effects of sin are everywhere. However, if we look at how things were back in Eden, before Adam and Eve were tempted, the Garden was as God intended.

We lose perspective because of the fall of man. He has given us the tools to get it back. God says to come to Him like a child. He promises to give us peace in any circumstance. He also tells us to, ". . . seek first His Kingdom and all these things will be added unto you." Matthew 6: 33. This is pretty awesome. He gives us a promise that His Son Jesus is coming again to reign. Even in tough times, God is practical.

Look at creation through the "practicality filter." Pick any area of creation that interests you and observe it through the lens of "creation justification"—*why* God made it *that* way. Let's look again at the sky. Stars help ships to navigate. The moon gives us a night light. The planets are benchmarks to measure seasons and time. How practical and orderly of God!

Everything was planned; from the celestial universe to the universe of our bodies. Our skin, for example, is very practical. It has several purposes. It gives our delicate organs a place of safety and holds us together. It makes us easier to look at (which helps in finding a mate), and the skin protects us from danger. The skin is designed with very practical receptors. These help to keep us from getting too close to a fire and tell us to get out of the cold.

> Catch the Godly passion and love exhibited through design. Disregard assumption-based ideas about Godless creation origins that distract us from truths about our Creator.

Our skin protects itself with repeated use by developing calluses. It gives us our individual identities. It comes in different colors, it changes color locally or overall to tell us there is a problem. It magically repairs itself when we get a scrape or cut. God gave our skin dynamic growing instructions. These precise instructions tell our skin what parts to close up and what parts to leave open. Our noses, mouths and ears allow entry for smells, food and sound. Our eye sockets provide a place for our eyes to view God's glorious world! Our skin provides the envelope for the *beauty* of our form to take shape. I think it's very nice of God to outfit us in a morphsuit; a literal skin onesie!

The skin is touch-sensitive. You can sooth a soul with gentle touch, or offer security, warmth and comfort. The muscles underneath it give skin form, grace and beauty.

Hair grows from it for many reasons. We can keep extra warm by letting hair grow long on our heads or faces. It conveniently regulates our body temperature. And, since there is such a variety of hair colors and styles, it helps us to have unique identities from one another.

Whatever makes your heart glad in Creation, examine it through the practicality filter. It is guaranteed to help improve your countenance! God was designing and thinking of us from His very first thoughts of Creation. Catch the Godly passion and love exhibited through design. Disregard assumption-based ideas about Godless origins that distract us from truths about our Creator. These human, finite concepts are merely passion distractions.

It is good to take time in prayer to thank Him for design and creativity. The passion God has for us shows us that He wants us to thoroughly exalt and acknowledge His creation and experience life in every sense of the word.

> *. . . They blessed the king and then went home, joyful*
> *and glad in heart for all the good things the LORD had*
> *done for his servant David and his people Israel.*

I Kings 8: 66

> *Through him all things were made; without him*
> *nothing was made that has been made.*

John 1: 3

The Creation acronym H.E.A.V.E.N. is simple and easy to memorize (Page 58). Perhaps you can create one of your own. We can easily spot H.E.A.V.E.N. in what we see. In our comings and goings, we should take time to explore books on favorite interests, nature, zoos, parks and gardens, and look through a telescope or a microscope. Life can get richer very quickly when we look at things a little closer!

A local university a offered a tour of their core facilities. The tour included visual samples of what their new research equipment could see. It was a very exciting event. This technology is providing new ways of examining, seeing and detecting. Local industry can take advantage of seeing things we've never seen before. Hence, encouraging invention, cures, and solutions to age old problems.

If you ever have an opportunity to visit a Microsculpture exhibit, it will entrance you. Or, you can visit the creator's website: microsculpture.net. Levon Bliss has patiently photographed colorful insects using a microscope lens, and a tracking and layering system to manage, on average, **2500** shots to make one super print. These prints are 3 meters in length. When shooting small objects close-up, the depth of field narrows greatly. Typically, this would make it difficult to see the insect's complete form with clarity. However, with this new technique, is that every scale, and follicle is in crystal clear focus.

Engage with God's many creations in ways you understand and can appreciate. When you get the message of creation, remember to compliment, thank Him for these things.

God gave us a proverbial candy store filled with multitudes of flavors to discover—*if* we pay attention to our curiosity! Explore and investigate, dissect and then piece back together, take apart and make connections. Next: combine, mix, agitate (meditate), water it, give it the acid test (or whatever test you can dream up), electrify it, shake it, stretch it, taste it, record it, play it, float it and fly it into outer space. You never know where God will help you land, but one thing is certain: It's going to be awe inspiring!

5
Diversity and Devotion

God was very intentional on the subject of diversity. Diversity covers the categories of creation while variety differentiates species, grouping or family. The big picture is stated in Genesis. The birds of the air, fish of the sea, animals, plants, stars, sky, sun, air, water, man, woman, earth and its natural resources, and energies are fully complete with many mysteries.

God didn't give us a gigantic tennis court floating in the cosmos to reside on, with evil on one side of the net and good on the other side.

If He did give instructions, God could have left a single-line instruction sheet that read, "Stay clear of the edges," but He didn't! He left us a highly creative, humorous, extremely amazing universe filled with mind-blowing variety, practicality and diversity, for everyone to enjoy! For an instruction manual, He left us the Bible—the inspired Word of God. The detail covered in the Bible is astonishing. It's not always cut and dried. We may think it is because of our worldview and limited wisdom. It could be deliberately designed that way to inspire debate, discussion or to challenge us in our faith.

> *And without faith it is impossible to please God, because anyone who comes to him must believe that he exists and that he rewards those who earnestly seek him.*
>
> Hebrews 11: 6 (NIV)

Diversity can be found in the make-up of our character. Our moods, temperaments and attitudes can sometimes get us into trouble. However, on the bright side, could these be instilled to push us to the end of ourselves? Perhaps they push us past the familiar into dependency. For example, when we are impatient, the frustration can trigger a disgruntled mood. When we find ourselves in a situation that is beyond our ability to solve, the discomfort can push into the face of God. Many of us have been there. When we are pleading for an answer or relief, this comes from the heart. That's right where God wants us.

In Ecclesiastes, King Solomon's countenance is revealed. Solomon, who was the son of King David, was blessed with every material possession possible—everything imaginable—including wisdom. His kingdom stretched from the

God didn't give us a gigantic tennis court floating in the cosmos to reside on, with evil on one side of the net and good on the other side.

Our moods, temperaments and attitudes can sometimes get us into trouble. However, on the bright side, could these be instilled to push us to the end of ourselves?

Euphrates River all the way down to Egypt. However, his quest for wisdom eventually drove him to despair. But in the end, God used Solomon to direct His people back to Himself.

King Solomon had everything a human could ask for; from cattle, horses and servants, to vast property and monetary means. But still, he searched for more. He was looking for purpose in life—the secret of existence. Solomon finally asks, "What is the meaning of it all?" Solomon surmises that all is meaningless. In Solomon's eyes, man works and then he dies, the sun rises and sets. . . redundantly. Even the natural elements, like the life-giving circulation of the air (winds) and water (streams) constantly repeat. This prompts him to complain that all things are wearisome! Remember, this King has it all, including wealth beyond anyone's wildest dreams! But it would seem that this wise man has quite a dreary outlook on life! The bottom line is,

Solomon has become a supreme pessimist; he doesn't live. He merely exists.

this king of the immense land of Israel, is quite bored! He shares that he is not fulfilled, adding that there is ". . . nothing new under the sun." Solomon bemoans nearly every other aspect of his life, as if to say why do we "bother living at all?" Solomon has become a supreme pessimist; he doesn't live—he merely exists, and does so without any dreams, without aspirations and is without any anticipation for what the future can bring.

However, as we explore God's creation, we will discover that God's Word will give us hope. First and foremost, there is a loving and passionate God who is building, or has built, a place for us to go after this life. God's Word helps us to get past the clutches of the enemy and to avoid Hell. We can immediately have peace of mind and heart! Are these things of God good? Are there things on earth more valuable than our souls? The discovery that we are loved and cherished should give us a glad heart, full of joy, and a broad grin! Is that not worth living for?

Solomon had a load of earthly possessions, but one thing he was missing was *perspective*. Somehow, in his reaching for the stars and seeing life in his own way, Solomon lost sight of God. Does that sound familiar?

> Somehow, in his reaching for the stars and seeing life in his own way, Solomon lost sight of God. Does that sound familiar at all?

Solomon chose to run after earthly wealth and other gods. He neglected to recognize the diversity in the beautiful world that God had created. Solomon did not have a grateful heart.

We do not know if Solomon fully recovered from his lost ways. However, he did point back to God by instructing his readers to "Fear God and Keep His commandments."[1] God used Solomon's temperament, attitude and moods for His own glory! Even in our disappointing and selfish human nature, God can bring us closer to His heart. Solomon's example was quite personal, but hopefully still beneficial. God shouts, "I Am" through the make-up of our character, too.

Words cannot even describe the scope of diversity that our Creator has given our planet. We have poisonous and edible berries, soft and hardwood trees, cloudy and sunny days and changing seasons. We have diverse energies to draw upon; coal, oil, wood, hydro-electricity, gas, oxygen, wind and the sun. In addition, He has gifted people with many diverse talents in the

> God is motivated purely out of the incredible love He has for us.

> God rejoices that His children can travel through this earthly dimension to a spiritual one and dock our souls to the Alpha and Omega.

arts and various areas of specialized knowledge. Thankfully, He has blessed many with spiritual gifts such as discernment, mercy, hospitality, an affinity for children, leadership or musical abilities.

So how can we shape our thoughts of diversity into a simple understanding which brings glory to God? If we can recall that, no matter what we are considering in creation, there is an active, loving Designer (God) behind each creation and that God is motivated purely out of the incredible love He has for us. He wants to get our attention, show His greatness, and warm our hearts enough to see us smile.

God rejoices that His children can travel through this earthly dimension to a spiritual one and dock our souls to the Alpha and Omega. If you can acknowledge that even one of the smallest specks of creation, a pollen particle, is designed by God, it is good. We have only touched on a small sampling of diversity. We can imagine the vast commitment and incomprehensibly *divine* devotion necessary to design the *diversity* that is present in our daily lives, and into life itself.

Devotion

Webster defines the word *devotion* as religious fervor, an act of prayer or private worship, a religious exercise or practice. A second meaning is an act of devoting—devotion of time and energy, or *a state of being ardently dedicated and loyal.* The third meaning has to do with the object of one's devotion.

Some of the synonyms include: adoring, affectionate, loving, fond, tender and tenderhearted.

We will just look at the second and third meanings. The example Webster gives here is, "a devotion of time and energy." Creation provides countless of examples of devotion for us to consider. The Emperor Penguin, living off the coast of Antarctica, is the epitome of familial devotion. They were designed with an instinct to protect their eggs to a point of sacrifice that is difficult to grasp. Once the female lays the egg, the male rests the egg on his feet for over two months while the female goes off to sea, to feed. The male waits in subzero temperatures and uses its time and energy to keep the egg warm. It does nothing else! The males huddle together and constantly walk in circles to generate body energy and to protect the new life from bitter temperatures and harsh Arctic winds. The male doesn't even eat during this time. Finally, after nearly 60 days, the female returns and shares her bounty.

In the same way, God asks us to consider another bird, the sparrow. He tells us He feeds them. Why does God care for these birds? After all, it's just a little bird, one of billions on the planet. But God is Holy and perfect in His care-giving. God tells us not to worry because if He cares for these little birds, He certainly will care for us. God is indeed devoted to us; we are children of the King!

Our heavenly Father has wired us for devotion! We can exhibit devotion to each other, to our children, to our families, and to Him! He designed this inner wiring and His devotion to us is *extreme*, as exhibited in His entire life-sustaining creation.

What intricate complexity it takes to be omnipresent; taking care of our physical, emotional and spiritual requirements! God created us with a personal will, that grants our individuality—our freedom to choose our eternal destiny. His engineering and planning laid the foundations of life. As earthly designers with human limitations, we can understand that thought is required prior to creating. But there was so much more. In fact, we may never see the entire picture until we reach heaven.

We're made in His image. God has given us the ability to understand thought. Scripture is clear that His "thoughts" of us outnumber the grains of sand. . . Psalm 139: 18, as this is the first part of creation. We should be satisfied with that. It gives us something to look forward to when passing from this life to the next: learning how God converts thought into tangible things.

In a past TV series called *Amazing Stories*, author and director Steven Spielberg made a valiant attempt to demonstrate an act of creating something out of nothing. One particular episode was titled "The Mission" and it included a very exciting rescue scene. During a nasty gunfight, a World War II ball turret gunner and aspiring cartoonist became trapped in the glass bubble on the plane's underside. In the course of the battle, the gun turret entry hatch became fused shut and the landing gear on the wings blew off. The men finished their mission and headed back to base to land.

> As earthly designers with human limitations, all we can understand is that thought is required prior to creating, before the work of "creating" commences.

The plane was running out of fuel and the men had to land. Everyone knew what the outcome would be with no landing gear. The gunner had a brand new family waiting for him back home. He had his sketchbook with him in the gun turret. As the plane made its final approach, Spielberg allowed the viewers to see the gunner thinking about his family and tears flowing down his face. It was a very emotional scene. Then, in his desperation to survive, he sketched feverously the WW II plane in which they were trapped. Then he added the wheel and landing gear where it should be on the wings. The camera zoomed in as he took his foundational sketch lines to expressive dark, heavy lines giving the landing gear its form and definition. He drew harder and faster, crying with passion as he worked, knowing somehow his life depended on it! Magically, the lines on the paper emerged under the wings of the plane and formed the complete landing gear just as he sketched it. Just then, the plane touched down and the drawing held until the plane stopped and they were able to break the hero free from the prison of his gun turret.

The gunner's devotion to his family, his determination, desperation, belief, and his powerful imagination gave birth

> There is a similar passion and *devotion* in mind for each of us, just as He "imagined."

to life saving reality in this colorful work of fiction. However, with God, the details, the symbiosis and marvel of it all, show similar passion and *devotion* in mind for each of us, just as He "imagined." We are *skillfully wrought* in creation.[2] Each of his creations is complete as He envisioned.

When it comes to creating something out of nothing, we can't cross the lines of emergence (the process of coming into being or appearing), no matter how hard we try. We are drawn that way, just as God intended. God even engineered people to be devotion-capable. Let's try to put that in an artist's sketchbook or on an

> God even engineered people to be devotion-capable. Let's try to put that in an artist's sketchbook or on an engineer's blueprint!

engineer's blueprint! In Dr. Caroline Leaf's recent work *Jump Start Your Brain,* she reveals that our positive, healthy thoughts create new thought pathways inside our brains. In contrast, scripture tells us that there is a "root" of bitterness, suggesting growth or change. She claims that "mind changes matter." A wonderful example of quantum physics aligning with scripture.

Dr. Mark Hyman, Director of the Cleveland Clinic Center for Functional Medicine uses epigenetics in healthy living. He teaches that gene function can change through behavior.

Our wiring, engineering, and everything we need on this life-sustaining planet are complete. That includes our emotions, thinking processes, and even our ability to make decisions. The extraordinary devotion God has for us is very apparent in the details of our design and the design of all creation.

God continued His devotion and expresses His love by giving us a garden. Not just any garden, but one with an expression reflective of His transcendent genius. He gave us millions of plants to explore, discover and enjoy. This garden offers us remarkable beauty, life giving oxygen, energy, food, recreation and utter amazement. The "garden" is a day to day reminder of the indescribable affection and passion that God has for us.

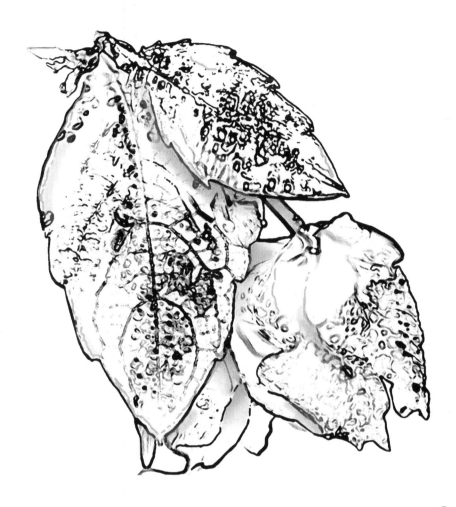

6
The Garden Around Us

There are two gardens, the Garden of Eden and our own "garden" around us. The Garden of Eden is our benchmark of things that were, and of things to come (a new earth in place without the devil's influence). The Garden of Eden was God's intended way of life for us, free from curses and sin—a paradise. Adam and Eve made choices representing their independent and sinful natures. Unfortunately, these earned them a one-way ticket through the exit door, into the unknown.

But, before you bemoan the actions of Adam and Eve, remember that we probably would have made the same decision if we were there! God knew this and the rest is history.

When the books of the Bible were written, they were written by inspired men of God. The people of the time worked the land and sea with their hands, basic tools, and resources. If a local newspaper were printed, a sample headline would read. . . "Since the advent of the plow and sickle. . ."

> The Garden of Eden was God's intended way of life for us, free from curses.

But before their fall, Adam and Eve didn't need tools. And if they had, the tools wouldn't break down! God didn't require them to toil by working the land for sustenance. The land was not yet cursed. There weren't any plant destroying insects, greedy gophers, misdirected deer, blight, disease, weeds, Canada thistle, frost, floods, or drought to worry about.

There were no wars against the elements, or invaders in the Garden of Eden. They picked and they ate! The atmosphere was like that of our humid greenhouses. Imagine how easy they had it! There was perfect order with each other and with God. He walked around with them and they knew the sound of His steps.

> *They heard the sound of the Lord God walk-*
> *ing in the garden in the cool of the day, . . .*
>
> Genesis 3: 8

Even the animals had pleasant dispositions. The wild wasn't wild yet!

If we could go back before the Garden of Eden, before the beginning. . . and look at the Designer's drawing board of plant life, it would be difficult to glean the incomprehensible depths of the creation process. As one who visualizes, I experimented with a photo I took in a garden. The result of one image was both accidental and astonishing. The leaves of the plant looked as though they were in a mixed designed and engineered state of creation. Shades of green appeared to be just coming into existence.

The color blue has long been symbolic of water or new birth. Water droplet outlines seem to represent a vascular pipeline for controlled water distribution critical for a leaf's existence. The intense oranges and reds looked like the energy map needed to transform nothing into something. The leaf veins seemed to appear as a foundational skeleton. Even the black represented the Creator's starting point on the leaf.

With each design, God had a separate mission in mind. One of the missions of the Garden was to provide the body with fuel. The body needs proteins, sugars, minerals, fiber, and nutrients to run at peak performance. Remember, there was no stock pile of raw elements to draw from; no science lab supply store to order from. God brought the vision straight from His mind to life and created everything He desired Himself. He generated all that was needed.

In order to go deeper into the subject, let's imagine that God has a sketchbook and some handy test tubes. Before the beginning, God might have said, "The fruit needs to be portable, because my people will be mobile." So, He to sketched an orange. Next He may have said, "I'll give a protective outer coating. I will call it. . . skin." (See the photo/scan on the back cover of this book). He might have sketched a peel of banana. "The size can vary but most items need to be easily consumed and lightweight," God may have said as He sketched an apple, then some grapes. "The fruiting plants and trees need to be established where people live." Next, God begins to sketch individual seeds in patterns that we recognize today. "Each ripened fruit should grow and contain plenty of seeds. The seed should be easy to harvest, store,

> With each design, God had a separate mission in mind.

transport and spread around. It must have three key control elements to begin growth and sprouting: water, soil, and sunlight. Without these things, the seeds remain dormant, but ready for spontaneous or planned growth. Imagine God making a close-up, cut-away drawing of soil layers with a sun and rain mix, in the background like we sometimes see today. Overlaying everything are dashed lines, representing the elements. God's pencil begins ghosting multiple colors out softly, like an airbrush. Some patterns seem random and some are orderly. For pollination, the Master Gardener has indicated an invisible radar which surrounds newly sprouted seedlings, almost like a plant-to-insect signal is being engaged.

God's drawing breaks out into a vast number of window-like panes, Each representing development requirements. The "engineering prints" look like animated holographic imagery with an unknown energy radiating and connecting other schematics within other drawings. All are rotating for 360° viewing. One layer has a familiar DNA strand, with a series of neutrinos branching off of it. (A sub atomic particle with the ability to move through matter.) These neutrinos move in and out of existence and are doing so apparently on the drawing. Another layer has honeycomb like illustration, with a myriad of equations surrounding it. One drawing is a typical bee, with wing, leg, and antenna entry points and tendon-like strands holding it all together, and arrows indicating blood flow direction. On another, an animation of the bee's heart chambers opening and closing. Gauge-like settings measure gravitational forces. More equations are on the next layer, along with measurements of wall thicknesses, wing speed settings and more ordered math symbols in a language unlike any other.

Another layer has Morse Code-like lines, again, with an unknown energy form mimicking the task of a bee, a blossom laden with pollen,

> The Master Gardener has indicated an invisible "radar" which surrounds newly sprouted seedlings, almost like a plant-to-insect signal is being engaged.

the airflow, and the pressure created above and below each wing seem to be indicated here.

God continues His work: "My people will need to eat and fuel their bodies. Hunger will alert them to eat. I will give them nerve sensations to tell them when they are full. I want them to experience joy when they eat. I'll give them taste buds—9000 of them![1] I will engineer a tongue to secure these taste buds and wire it to the brain so people can distinguish flavor—loads and loads of them! This tongue will also be used to formulate words, which they will use to communicate with one another and with me."

"I will let them be truly creative with access to a wide variety of plant species. Along with the tongue, I will give them a nose, which has the ability to differentiate between spoiled and fresh foods. Defined pleasure receptors will react positively to the aroma of exquisite foods."

"The edible plants need to be tasty on the tongue, and the non-edible, not so. Three ounces of saliva per minute will help deliver the food and initiate the digestive process. Fruit will change colors, so my people will know when the fruit is ready to eat. When they are done with the skins and cores they can be returned to the earth and replenish the ground."

God thought about the needs of our bodies in depth: A very small sampling would include:

"The body will need vitamin C and potassium along with fiber and natural water. The banana and orange will be perfect for this. Now to engineer the trees that will have ability to bear this kind of fruit, I'll create blossoms to attract the bees for pollination and to tell them fruit is on its way! I need something to flavor up all the wheat and grains they will use. Tomatoes will suffice. People can slice, dice and boil them down to place on future wheat and potato sticks (noodles and french fries)."

He designed a diverse cornucopia of foods for us to choose from: "Watermelon, pumpkin, squash, cucumber, beans, peppers, radishes, lettuce, spinach, cabbage, garlic, celery, strawberries, raspberries, blueberleries, avocado, pears, plums, cherries, and of course, the apple, pineapple, coconut, lemon and lime. . . I'll make these too. The huge variety along with plant-based spices will make eating a very delightful experience. They will be happy to learn that the variety contains most of their needed nutrients.

I will build in wonderful surprises that they will discover. The lemon will preserve the avocado, the garlic will be an energy source, the oils from coconuts will condition dry skin and help with blood flow. After they discover flour, and learn that they can bake fruit with it, they will be in pie paradise!

"People will need help to see there is more to life than meets the eye. Many will discover that *invisible* forces are at work in and throughout creation.[2] When they develop the technology to see My future surprises: the molecule and the subatomic, it will inspire them to look to Me in childlike wonder, and offer thanks. It will compel them to discover more about Me."

Each of these aforementioned garden-grown sumptuous wonders has a design story, objective, and purpose. All these have been initiated into existence[3] to be thoroughly enjoyed by us![4] God was very thoughtful to design these foods for us to fully savor, in and out of the Garden of Eden!

Weeds, argh, are the gardener's enemy and teacher. The good Lord wanted us to experience this first hand for several reasons; one was to help us to better understand

> "After they discover flour, and learn that they can bake fruit with it, they will be in pie paradise!"

> Messages get across more clearly when your hands get dirty, your body becomes exhausted and your spirit is challenged.

> The harm is not above the surface, but below it, where you can't see until you go weeding.

certain aspects of the Bible. For example, we read parables about weeds, farming and soil. Then, we learned about the challenges (or post-fall curses, thanks to Adam and Eve) in working the land and toiling by the sweat of our brows, as God admonished Adam, in Genesis. We learn that reading and doing are very different. Messages get across more clearly when your hands get dirty, your body becomes exhausted and your spirit is challenged! Being close to the earth can be quite enlightening.

> Do not let the worries of the world choke you like weeds.

The foxtail looks like a harmless blade of grass with a bushy tail on its end. It is easy to think that the foxtail is not causing problems. However, the harm is not above the surface, but below it, where you can't see until you go weeding. When you pull on the stem, a basketball-sized root system comes out! Next to a tomato plant root system, this secret invader will choke out your precious plant, or kill it completely.

> You literally have to declare war to defend your crops.

This is a good example of how God is talking to us through the garden. He states in His word:

> . . . but the worries of this life,
> the deceitfulness of wealth and
> the desires for other things
> come in and choke the word, making it unfruitful.

Mark 4:19 (NIV)

Do not let the worries of the world choke you like weeds. However, the foxtail was not the only plant-threatening villain to visit us. Another weed that causes horror is Canada thistle. This weed grows fast and is very hardy. Its' needled stems and leaves make them untouchable with bare hands, and it plagued our property with a vengeance. We talked with farmers, extension agents, organic-growers, and no one had an easy answer for how to rid these from our fields. And we had *hundreds* of them! An Amish farmer suggested brushing on a special natural chemical onto each leaf of the weed! Really? Another grower said to burn them!

> # Evil is unleashed, and if you are going to beat evil, you can never give up!

What's nasty about these weeds is that they have a horizontal root system with a 12'–18' reach! They spread like wildfire! They made weeding very difficult, choked out the good plants, they were inedible to livestock and they couldn't be touched by bare hands without penalty! Just when you think you have gotten the best of them, the new shoots emerge. You literally have to declare war to defend your crops!

> Design requirements of plant molecules include: formability, a memory bank to hold growing instructions, a mini-nutrient and flavor lab, sun reactivity, water-drawing capabilities and even a seasonal behavior clock.

The spiritual lesson we glean is that evil is unleashed. And if you are going to beat evil, you can never give up. This is the recipe for a fruitful garden and this is the strategy to beat earth's enemy! The ground is full of enemies that would kill the fruits of your labor and steal their precious resources; the sun, the nutrients from the soil and even take their place in your field, all the while causing you heartache and pain. Is the devil that prowls around like a ravenous lion as he waits to devour us any different? But we are not alone in our struggles. In fact, God gives us His word that He will never leave us or forsake us.

Care and Provision

Have you ever witnessed the astounding miracle of plant growth and photosynthesis? Without the oxygen that plant life supplies, the human race could not survive. The realization of all the incredible things that God does every single day in a garden should cause us to be filled with amazement!

We need to break out the test tubes to truly consider plant functions. God created life-giving molecules. God engineered DNA, atoms and ions, for starters. Some of the design requirements of plant molecules include: formability, a memory bank to hold growing instructions (like the ins and outs of pollination), a mini-nutrient and flavor lab, sun reactivity, water-drawing capabilities, and even a seasonal behavior clock. All this design and engineering of growth instruction had to be in molecules smaller than a pinpoint!

Two fascinating examples of this intricate design are the watermelon and pumpkin. From something so relatively small, these two giants develop, and epitomize the flavors of summer or fall, respectively.

God provided for us through the garden. He also cares and provides for the garden itself. Think about the vines of these fruits. They are one half-inch in diameter and carry everything the fruit needs to live. The blossoms are astounding, in that they somehow have an internal time clock, which causes them to make use of the morning dew and to pollinate.

> God has programmed a "command center" into all living things.

In a city near here, a business called Rockwell International employs electrical engineers, mechanical engineers and computer scientists to program manufacturing equipment. These specialists program the machines. Programs instruct the machines to perform various tasks. These tasks include: what temperature, how long to hold the temperature, when to change the temperature, and when to end the task. The commands are almost endless. The capabilities of these *man-made* machines are fantastic!

Like these engineers and scientists, God has programmed a "command center" into all living things. The squash family has a yellow die injection-system for the plant's blossoms. These bright blossoms attract bees to pollinate them. The blossom pedals are so delicate that a strong wind will tear them. They open and close as if on cue. There are both male and female flowers. Each has a specific job.

> How can there be any question as to the deep forethought required to produce such intricate vegetation mechanics?

Because of their fragility and fertility make-up, the female flowers need protection from predators and the heat of the sun in the early weeks of development. A dozen flowers may emerge, but only a few will develop fruit. The thin vines are engineered to produce giant, umbrella-like leaves to cover shorter, fragile female flowers. How can there be any question as to the deep forethought required to produce such intricate vegetation mechanics?

The male flower is engineered to grow higher than the one-foot leaf canopy. His pollen-coated anther attracts the bees from afar, but this also attracts the deadly cucumber beetle. This design can cause enough of a distraction above the canopy to allow the discrete pollination process to happen under cover.

If fruit has been produced, the baby pumpkin or watermelon will require lots of water. The wonder vine (that is more like a tiny stick at this stage) gets a little bigger, but can't quite keep up with the water demands, so out pop tendrils (the curly-cue things that decorate Cinderella's pumpkin carriage). These are actually water augmenting, ground-boring vine tendrils and they are hard at work. These spinney little things drill into the ground and draw water to the vine.

I'd like to see any human being attempt to engineer and design all that on a pinhead!

Sweat of the Brow

We can see that God did the fantastic and glorious design engineering of these plants. Today, mankind is still trying to find the control box in the vine that initiates all the perfectly timed creation commands!

We have been created with an innate drive to protect the source of our sustenance. Sweating begins with fear of the unknown. The anxiety comes from not knowing what may lurk in the fields. What labor is required to conquer anything that threatens to destroy our work. More unknowns include airborne micro-bombs like blight and visible plagues like powdery mildew. All the while, life-lesson-analogies begin to take root—a well designed plot is in the making.

People who are not farmers think that once the plant is growing the work is done! Now all you have to do is water it and sit back and wait until harvest time! Not true!

Soon, the dreaded invaders appear, like the Hornworm. It looks like some kind of alien, five-inch-long, green caterpillar-Dachshund mix, with a pointy tail! In a matter of days, it can decimate an entire crop. Some may assume deer enjoyed the produce as an evening salad bar, but later learn it was this insidious caterpillar! The Hornworm comes prepared for his secret mission of destruction, completely camouflaged with the exact color of a tomato plant leaf. To find them, listen for the crunch of their jaws slicing through the tender plants as they drive across the field. The sound is unmistakable.

> Mankind is still trying to find the control box in the vine that initiates all the perfectly timed creation commands.

Another example of the farmer's toils, predicted in the book of Genesis, is blight. Blight occurs if the moisture is too high and the temperature drops too low. Blight is an invisible disease doing its evil deed. It can wipe out entire fields of tomato plants in less than five days, if not treated.

We may think the sweat of the brow ends with plowing and planting. Farmers must remedy these situations quickly, or the plants will fail. Remedies may include: plucking, spraying, wiping, squishing, and, worst off all, doing all of these tasks while bouncing around on a tractor, or stooped over in the heat of the sun or in the rain. Many times the only way to eliminate the threat is to crawl around in the dirt on our knees. This toil will help us appreciate heaven all the more!

> This toil will help us to appreciate Heaven all the more!

In the present days of modern conveniences, it is easy to forget that our ancestors were forced to deal with how quickly produce can perish. The first thing on their minds, we can be sure of, was *not* to put the newfound veggies in a two-door frigde! They quickly discovered another use for the cave with its cool temperatures.

Once the days of harvest arrive, the farmer's brow is again covered in perspiration. He will rush to enroll in the local farmer's markets to sell his produce before it goes bad. He will have to prepare for the market by purchasing scales, have the scales audited, buy tables, signs, umbrellas, etc. If he doesn't own a truck, he will ask friends and neighbors to lend him one. He will need to buy containers, pick the produce, pack the containers, price them, set up his booth, talk to customers, and encourage them to buy his produce. Usually, by noon or so, most farmers take down their display, unpack, dispose of the "unsellables," and repeat the entire process again for each market. We should never question the price of a tomato again from a local farmer! His *sweat of the brow* is done on our behalf! He is managing the garden around us! Thank you farmers! Maybe the real roots of celebrating Thanksgiving is that the farmers are thankful that the season is finally over! And we give a *healthy* "thank you" to our Master Gardener Creator that we have the ability to keep our bellies full with just the right ingredients!

> Gratitude is one of the greatest Christian graces;
> ingratitude, one of the most vicious sins.
>
> Billy Graham, Evangelist

Perfection

The life cycle is in motion, preparing, plowing and planting. The plants are sprouting from a seed, then producing fruit and, finally, decaying. Each garden element at any given time is in a state of change. All are designed *intentionally* for life-sustaining order and energy for our bodies. Along the way, God wants His children to enjoy all that He has made: A garden so perfect that it involves a three-part symbiosis that joins man, seed, and God. It was perfect in function then as it is now, in spite of the challenges the farmer faces.

> God designed this garden for *us*; to capture our imagination and to prompt us to wonder about the invisibles of life.

God designed this garden for *us*; to capture our imagination, and to prompt us to wonder about the invisibles of life. He wets [WRETS] our appetite with the promise of a curse-free garden to come. In reading about and experiencing this garden, we can draw analogies for shepherding, guiding and leading. We can gain new insights on discipline and perspective.

We enjoy physical, mental and spiritual health. In God's garden, there is rest, reflection and restoration.

Before the beginning, extremely complex ideas and concepts, with much consideration to heart related passions, were on life's drawing board.

Before the beginning, extremely complex ideas and concepts, with much consideration to heart related passions were on life's drawing board. This divine mix of mass-energy equivalence formulas and directives interplay with millions, of sub-atomic clusters lying in wait. The emergence of the tangible will connect built-in information streams designed to deliver time-sensitive, life-giving commands. These life-receiving creations stand ready to engage the photosynthesis process. All of this was designed and engineered with perfection, before the beginning, *simply waiting on the breath of life to come.* God's handiwork and His loving care in design are something special to consider and to meditate upon. Our worship would rise to heaven's gates if we would simply let the shouts of creation and the bigness of God echo in our hearts.

> Our worship would rise to heaven's gates if we would simply let the shouts of creation and the bigness of God echo in our hearts.

Biomimicry

Creation offers a plethora of inspiration. Hats off to The University of Akron. They are the first university offering an undergraduate certificate in biomimicry. "The Biomimicry Research Innovation Center (BRIC) is dedicated to connecting scientists, engineers, designers and businesspeople to catalyze biomimicry-based innovation. BRIC's vision is for biomimicry to become a driver for sustainable economic development in Northeast Ohio and beyond." Their website is https://www.uakron.edu/bric/. One fascinating application of biomiciry is in SWARM technology. It's a little creepy but a great example of what can be discovered by considering creation for inspiration.

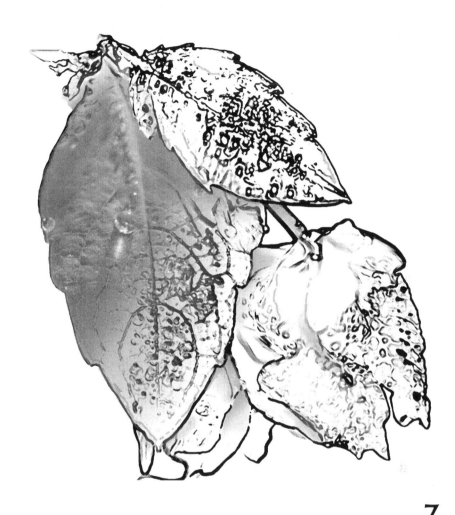

7

1.2 oz–2,000 lb Beasts

Our Creator went to a lot of trouble so we can enjoy a good steak, burger, roast and corned beef sandwich! Do you see the creativity of the bovine in the soccer shoes, baseball gloves and leather jackets we might use in everyday life? Some of our largest industries are built around this noble beast—the cow. Perhaps McDonalds® [1] wouldn't be who they are today if they were based on a hog or a tuna fish. And when you explore all of the uses this multi-functioning creature provides, once again, you should experience some shock and awe! How many people reach for cream in the morning for their cup of tea or coffee? Milk with chocolate—a symbiosis bar none (pun intended) shakes, cakes, puddings and cream pies are all cow depend@nt! Where would the salad, or cracker or chip be without cheese? We dip with it; we smother with it, age it, smoke it, grate it and shake it. It's a flavor that tantalizes our taste buds!

> # Shakes, cakes, puddings and cream pies are all cow dependant!

How many of us can down a quart of ice cream in a matter of minutes? froYo, Dairy Queen® and Ben and Jerry®[2] would be lost without the cow! Lone Star® would be lonely without this hoofed wonder. Outback®[3] would be held back without the Black Angus beauties.

Nothing else converts green grass into ground-round like a cow! Cow basics include a flyswatter tail, four-stomach, cud-chewing digestive system, a 13.5 gallon daily water-injection system (saliva), a highly random manure spreading system to help fertilize the fields, and a growth rate of 60 to 1,200 lbs or more in 18 months, just on grass alone!

Like our pets, cows like a treat, in this case—sweet feed! I thank God for this, because cows naturally like to eat the grass on the other side of the fence and they sometimes escape. When they escape, it can create dangerous situations, but God gave us the ability to tame and control these massive creatures. When cows see a feed bucket, they come walking (or sometimes running), which makes it relatively easy to lead them back to pasture or back to the barn for the night. I have actually seen cows that are so happy that they frolic, like puppies shown a stick. It is a little nerve-racking to have a 1,200 lb creature happily kicking up its hooves as it races past you.

> # Nothing else converts green grass into ground-round like a cow!

Another instinct God designed is that cows seem to want to obey. In raising them, I had the personal relief in seeing them obey a "stop" hand signal in the middle of a stampede (I am thankful I did not die in the midst of that demonstration). The cows did this without attending a single cow obedience class! God made them to pay attention to us. When they don't pay attention, there are some dog breeds that know how to get them to obey. God made the cows corral capable!

In fact, The Creator made many creatures that defy physics and biology. These living things could not function in a phase of their own evolution. Examining how these creatures operate, it is clear to see they were designed to function just the way they do today.

Animals That Challenge Us!

Let's look at one of these animals Dr. Job Martin mentions in his *Incredible Creatures That Defy Evolution DVD I*. In the case of the giraffe, Martin points out that it would "take a great pressurized pump to pump blood over six feet straight up through the giraffe's neck to get to the giraffe's brain." The same pressure necessary to pump the blood

up six feet to the brain would explode it when the giraffe bent down to drink. But God designed a solution for that.

What makes the design of the giraffe's neck so awesome is that it has six valves in it. Each valve closes consecutively as the giraffe lowers his head. Furthermore, the giraffe wouldn't be able to stay down long enough to finish a drink of water before passing out if it weren't for a "sponge" at the end of his spine that compensates for the shutoff valves by supplying the needed blood. This balances its equilibrium, so the giraffe is able to lift its head very rapidly without passing out and make a quick getaway from predators. Dr. Martin uses this example, as well as many others, to show the necessity of completed designs for animals to survive.[15] A half developed or half evolved giraffe could not survive its first drink of water let alone reproduce. An underdeveloped valve system in the giraffe's neck would explode the brain. More importantly, there are no fossil records verifying these transitions of macroevolution. The correct design had to be in place from the first giraffe.

Looking closely at the design of the giraffe, we see a passionate designer. God's love is expressed here. The giraffe is beautiful in design and color. It has a very unusual shape. Each of the giraffe's spots are unique, just like our fingerprints. It's stomach has four chambers to digest the lofty vegetation. It is the tallest animal on the planet and was made intentionally to reach great heights. It has the long legs to go with the long neck. It even has furry horns atop its lofty perch, perhaps only to make his face look very silly and very friendly. Children giggle in amazement at these creatures. What practical purpose does the giraffe serve except to amaze us? Perhaps God did this so we could grasp the magnificence of His handiwork in our human minds. Why would God do this? The answer is simple: To create awe is a practical thing for God to do. As part of His unfathomable plan to establish a relationship with us, He proclaims Himself the supreme and sovereign God who set everything—*every living thing*—into motion, before time began.

> To create awe is a practical thing for God to do.

Giant Sea Boogie Monster. At a first glance this creature appears to look like an abandoned parachute that is inhabited by a giant snail. Steven Haddock, a scientist for the Monterey Bay Aquarium Research Institute in Moss Landing, CA, says the mysterious creature is a *deepstaria enigmatica* jellyfish. It's translucent, has honeycomb-like internal tissue cell structure, can turn itself inside out, and has an arm-like organ that comes in handy (pun intended). A video shot, April 25, 2012, reveals the mysterious creature of the deep, resting at about 5,000 feet down next to an oil well pipe. This particular jellyfish was captured on video by Oceanic. Naturally curious *deepstaria enigmatica* jellyfish hardly seems to function under its' own command. It looks like a ghost-like, hooded transformer, with very few parts. If it could not undulate so magnificently, it would likely sink to the bottom and die. The graceful movements are vital to its existence.

Other intriguing jellyfish features include: an internal electricity production and storage facility, an erythematic, light-pulse trans-

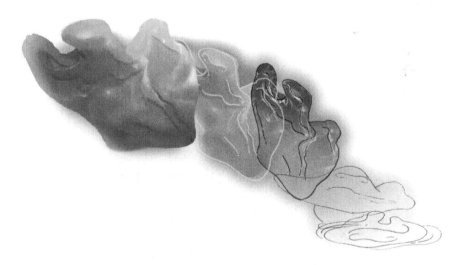

former and a self-defense, electrical-discharge taser unit that can stun or kill upon contact. The purpose of this jellyfish has yet to be discovered; the *enigmatica* is a mystery. God created these just because He could. Perhaps God wanted to offer us the challenge to explore to find out more about it. Search this video online and be amazed. *link or web address?*

Mimic Octopus. The name says it all! This creature can mimic 15 other species of animals. The built-in knowledge, along with an extremely clever instinct, makes this eight-legged sea serpent something to reflect on.

> One might even have been able to hear a zany movie quote coming from God's Creation lab, "It's so crazy... it just might work!"
>
> Pistachio Disguisey
> in the movie
> *The Master of Disguise*

The anatomical features and responsive molecular structure designed into this *one* creature is astounding. Think about it: The ocean does not come with full-size mirrors to practice impressions! In an interview, the comedian Jim Carrey said that many of his early years were spent in front of a mirror contorting his face into celebrities such as James Cagney or Clint Eastwood, or just exploring "where no man has gone before" with his face. He would spend hours in front of a mirror getting the morph and mission just right.[4] The mimic octopus gets its impersonations right the first time without practicing in the

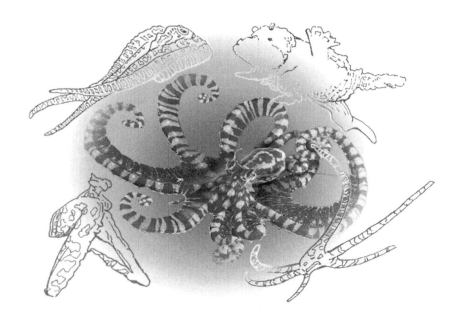

mirror. Some of the animals it mimics include; the flounder, lionfish, sea snake, stingray, and it can even transform itself to look like a turkey with human legs! It can also change color and texture to instantly match the environment. And it squirts the usual octopi dye (necessary predator protection camouflage).

Dana Carvey, in the humorous family friendly movie, *Master of Disguise*, played the part of a human chameleon. He changed from turtle guy, to cherry pie, to cow pie without missing a beat! He did this with the full capacities of creative thinking and with the help of a prop and a costume design shop. Our mimic octopus needed to be complete in design from the moment it appeared in the ocean in order to pull off performances such as these. If it failed in a half-developed presentation, it would simply be eaten. At

> The mimic octopus gets its impersonations right the first time without practice in the mirror.

that point, it could not genetically pass on its "learn how not to be eaten" experience. I can see God designing the mimic octopus and having a lot of fun with it! One might even have been able to hear a zany movie quote coming from God's Creation lab, "It's so crazy. . . this will boggle their minds for years." So next time you dig into your calamari and get one of those tentacles stuck to the roof of your mouth, remember the mimic octopus and it's' wondrous Creator!

Bombardier Beetle. This insect reveals God's nano technology at its best. The bombardier beetle is a miniature traveling chemical mixing plant and army tank wrapped up in one tough little package! This half-inch bug makes up its own hydrogen peroxide and hydroquinones to make smoking, caustic benzoquinones. This chemical explodes out at 212° F through rotating turret-style twin nozzles with precise, bull's-eye accuracy, on demand. This design offers a safe containment system along with an inhibitor—another control chemical. If this bug were half-developed through an evolutionary process, we would have a containment breech and the bug would dissolve itself![5] This defense system would need to be securely intact with all systems hot to function properly. This little bug blows away any of man's understandings through its highly sophisticated

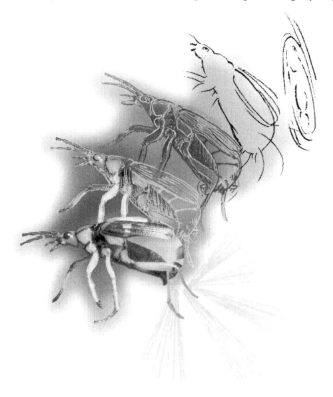

engineering, while pointing its inception to an extreme Designer.

Volcano Blind Shrimp. Geologist Bramley Murton from the RRS James Cook states:[6]

> "On the ocean floor at a volcano opening, temperatures can reach 750° F, heating water to the point where it can melt lead. The blazing hot, mineral-rich water is expelled into the icy cold of the deep ocean, creating a smoke-like effect and leaving behind towering chimneys of metal ore, some two story's tall. The spectacular pressure—500 times stronger than the earth's atmosphere—keeps the water from boiling."

Murton points out creatures that survive in spite of impossible circumstances:

> "The environment may appear brutal: the intense heat and pressure combines with toxic metals to form a highly acidic undersea cocktail. But vents host lush colonies of exotic animals such as hairy worms, blind shrimp and giant white crabs."

Murton states that the environment appears "brutal." While this habitat may serve these particular beings quite well, for us, de-

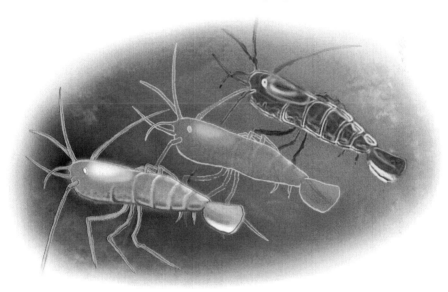

scribing this environment as brutal is an understatement. These temperatures alone melt lead! In these conditions, the tissue of any other animal would become completely annihilated. Yet, these animals are thriving. This is beyond physics and biology as we traditionally know it! As God spoke to Job to adjust his perspective, likewise God may be adjusting our perspective by exhibiting divine genius in His creation.

For since the creation of the world, God's invisible qualities, His eternal power and divine nature, have been clearly seen, being understood from His workmanship, so that men are without excuse. For although they knew God, they neither glorified Him as God nor gave thanks to Him, but they became futile in their thinking and darkened in their foolish hearts.

Romans 1: 20–21 (BSB)

The Angler Fish. Fishing is a way of life for many and it can mean many things to many people—from pleasure to employment. For the angler fish, it means survival. This is one of the few light-producing animals on

the planet. It has a very practical tool for attracting prey. This fish was designed to live about a mile down on the ocean floor, in complete darkness. There is a light on the end of a narrow extension that is attached to the top if its head. You might say it's more suited for an intimate, candlelit dinner for two! The only problem with that idea is that the guest just happens to be the main course! The pole also has a bait formation at the end of it. The light leads the way and attracts its prey.

Another major difference between angler fish and other fish is that it doesn't have buoyancy control. No swim bladder specifications can be found in the blueprints of this fish. The prominent bait and pole displayed in the shallows would make the angler fish an easy target and it would likely not survive if it had a swim bladder. The blueprint is complete and accurate just as God intended.[7]

The European Green Woodpecker. When this neighborhood exterminator makes his daily feeding rounds, he is actually keeping our trees healthy. God demonstrates His love for us from the tip of this

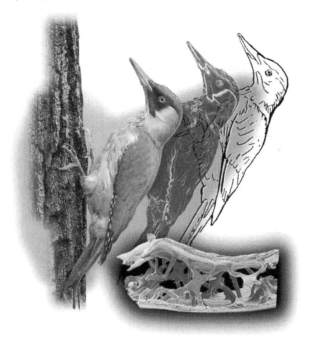

bird's tree-grabbing toes to its cute little drumming nose. The woodpecker's beak is unlike any other beak in strength. If other birds had to hammer like this, the results would be less favorable. A canary's beak would collapse. A chickadee beak would be chiseled away. A sparrow's beak would be splintered. But when purpose is considered in the creation design process, God understood that there was a need for a very strong, precision-built, 5-in-1-bug retrieval tool. This mechanism drilled, grab insects and grubs, and using that same beak it had to breathe! Another design requirement was the tongue. It's long tongue retraction system recoils around the head from top to bottom. The green woodpecker's tongue has barbs on the tip to drag its prey back through very small tunnels, all the while excreting special glue that holds the prey, but avoids gluing the bird's mouth shut! God designed the woodpecker's head to be protected from constant impact by including a special impact absorbing cartilage as part of the structure (quite a demonstration of mercy for this little creature). And for fun, God adds brilliant green coloring in the feathers for decoration. The bird has an incredible migration system, feather stabilizers for tree perching and an extra toe on the back part of the foot for clutching tree branches! All but two of the woodpecker species have the extra toe.[8]

> God understood that there was a need for a very strong, precision-built, 5-in-1 bug retrieval tool.

> As God spoke to Job to adjust his perspective, likewise God may be adjusting our perspective by exhibiting divine genius in His creation.

> If we look at this bird through the eyes of our Creator, we see another reason for its existence.

Australian Incubator Bird (Mallee-fowl). This particular species of ground dwelling bird looks sort of like a 3.5–4 lb. turkey. What's so unique about this bird is its uncanny ability to regulate temperature and humidity within its nest. The nest size is unbelievably large—about 20 feet across and has been seen to be as high as 50 feet! It also goes down about three feet into the earth. The nest is made and managed by the male. Sometimes multiple nests are made if the female isn't quite satisfied with the first construction the poor fellow has assembled. The Malleefowl dedicates nine months to a year building and maintaining this large incubation mound of soil, leaves and twigs. The Malleefowl maintains a mound temperature of 91° to 99.5° F and controls humidity by using its beak as a thermometer and hygrometer. They also can adjust the soil cover

to either retain or expel heat from the egg chamber by digging out soil or adding it.

The egg is almost the size of an ostrich egg. This comes from a four pound bird! When the egg hatches, the chick lies on its back and starts to scratch at the ceiling. Debris falls on its chest. Undaunted, it simply gives a shake and scratches again and repeats this escape process, which continues for up to three days. Talk about perseverance!

The survival rate with the Malleefowl is less than 2%. All this effort to break free from the confines of the eggshell, and in the next phase of its life, there is little chance of survival due to predators. According to the Malleefowl Preservation Group, this rare Australian bird is currently threatened by extinction.[9]

This story may mean different things to different people. We should be in awe just thinking about this amazing beak. How can this boney material measure temperature and humidity? This bird is designed with extremely accurate sensors that are "wired" to the brain, and the bird responds faithfully, time and time again. We humans can study the Malleefowl and discover usable scientific information, but if we look at this bird through the eyes of our Creator, we see another reason for its existence. Perhaps this bird was created to declare in a loud voice that no man can know the mysteries of God! It stands as a testimony to absolute (not accidental) *perfection* in design. For example, if the baby bird were to start scratching down like a chicken, it would never make it out of the nest and would ultimately die. It instinctively knows in which direction to dig and it knows not to give up! The design and foundational work of these animals is complete and astonishing.

> From the deceiver's point of view, it's somewhat comical or pathetic.

Peacock Spider. Nicknames include Sparklemuffin, Skeletorus and Elephant. These hilarious arachnids have eight legs and 5mm furry bodies. They come full of vibrant color and iridescent scales. Although scientists first discovered peacock spiders in the 1800s, they went virtually unstudied after a series of papers in the late 1950s In 2005, Jurgen Otto propelled them to spider fame and into people's hearts with his close-up photos. Peacock Spiders are on top of nature's most entertaining animals. They dance, hop, wiggle and shake for defense, mate attraction and, our amusement.

What's absolutely amazing is the tail. The illustration shows the different designs and faces that appear upright when the spider raises its tail. Its four eyes are in-line with its arms. Perhaps the Aboriginal peoples in Australia got their face painting and makeup ideas from these tiny arachnids.

Their eyes and face-like designs come in a variety of shapes, sizes, colors, and patterns. The creative work is deliberate and sophisticated. In some designs you can spot two different face motifs.

Could He have put these mysterious, mind-boggling animals in our midst to utterly blow away our traditional, finite thinking minds?

You can't use half-created or partially evolved raw elements to create something. The elemental design must be fully intact for them to have these complete behavioral properties. Half-developed carbon, nitrogen, phosphorus, oxygen, sulfur and half developed neurons or atoms with a half-baked strong force wouldn't do it either. These and other raw elements need to be fully complete to function. Like a fully developed animal, if they are not complete to begin with, they would not survive. If not fully

functional, if the mechanisms these animals use to escape predators were not already fully functional, they would not escape and they would be eaten. If they are eaten, evolution cannot take place.

The passing of time in and of itself cannot create. All matter and energy breaks down over time. Organic things always rot. If an attic full of junk sat for a million years, it would turn to a pile of dust. To believe that a higher ordered form will eventually emerge from the piles of dust is the core concept of evolution. From the deceiver's point of view, it's either comical or pathetic, that the devil is attempting to mock God. If he were to comment on this it might sound like, "Look what some of the educated people believe in! They are easily deceived. I can get them to believe in the ludicrous—instead of understanding deterioration, I will get them to believe that the natural law of atrophy will 'over time,' result in perfect-ordered creation. Watch, I will use *their self-perceived strengths of intelligence* to blind, not only themselves, but others." The common phrase: "You can't see the forest through the trees" couldn't ring truer.

> Creation brings many of us to our senses. It drives us to consider and acknowledge God, and can force us to humbly get out of the way.

The pressing issue is to identify the deception and its source. God is challenging our prideful, self-sufficient attitudes by putting these mysterious, mind-boggling animals in our midst to utterly blow-away our traditional, finite thinking minds.

Pride is difficult to recognize, let alone overcome. Creation brings many of us to our senses. It drives us to consider and acknowledge God, and can force us to humbly get out of the way and recognize that we are the children of an amazing, indescribable Creator God who loves us with a passion beyond measure!

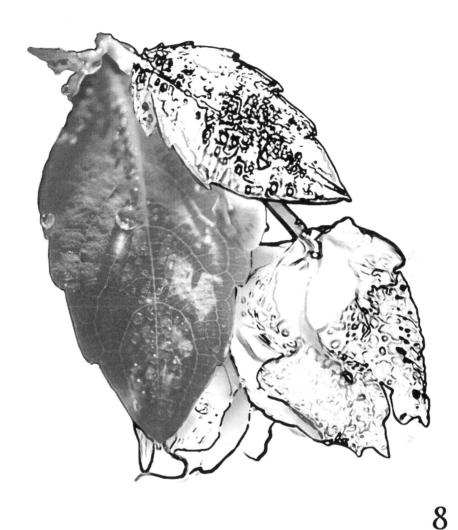

8

The Masters and Masterpieces

A masterpiece is something that was created, developed or discovered by someone, which others have established as rare and of high value. In many areas of life, we have granted individuals the title of being a master. The arts, sciences, geology, physics, painting, music, drama—even a sharp shooter—can achieve the skill level of master. The question we must ask ourselves is, Were the earthly masters and geniuses of history, self-made creators and thinkers, or were they divinely inspired?

Jesus stated that we would be doing greater works than these:

> *I tell you the truth, anyone who has faith in me will*
> *do what I have been doing. He will do even greater*
> *things than these, because I am going to the Father.*

John 14: 12 (NIV)

Maybe its not one or the other, maybe it's a little of both.

In *The Book of Genius*, Tony Buzan and Raymond Keene made the world's first attempt to rank the top ten geniuses of history. They included:

10.   Albert Einstein
9.   Phidias (architect of Athens)
8.   Alexander the Great
7.   Thomas Jefferson
6.   Sir Isaac Newton
5.   Michelangelo
4.   Johann Wolfgang von Goethe
3.   The Great Pyramid Builders
2.   William Shakespeare
1.   Leonardo Da Vinci

Each of these "greats" has created awe-inspiring work. When created works deviate from what we know or that which is familiar, we consider that it was divinely inspired and has the fingerprint of THE master. Through the works of these artists, God makes Himself evident. What about the rest of us less inspired people? Even J.K. Rowling, the author of the very successful *Harry Potter* series, shared that what troubled her most was that she felt she was an impostor—just a regular person—and not the genius that the world was making her out to be.[1]

When I worked on a design project for a large lighting manufacturer, I remember calling the inventor of some innovative 3D software. One of the first commercial users of this software was a very well known animated movie production company. The software was so successful that one of the demo projects is still part of their logo today. When the software came out, it boasted texture mapping and included recognition of light-source and shadow. These software features give the graphics a photorealistic appearance. The software even has an organic plant-growth mode! You set some end-result parameters and the software generates virtual growing branches, stems and leaves! As an artist, this new capability blew my understanding of the norm. Drafting boards would soon become obsolete, and it was the beginning of the end of hand painted cell animation.

> When created works deviate from what we know or that which is familiar, we consider that it was divinely inspired and has the fingerprint of THE master.

Questions filled my mind. Who can possibly think like this? Is he real? With this type of creative ability, I had to meet him! After just a few phone calls, we were able to connect. The first thing I asked the inventor was how he could create something so fantastic? He was very kind and modest. He said, "It was no big deal, just simple math equations." Yeah, easy for him, but *I* have never had a clue on where to begin the designing of such a tool! I realized that this would change the playing field entirely. And it has! Today, at least a third of the movies produced are fully digitally created, and a majority of them use this inventive technology for special effects. Whenever and wherever visualization needs to happen, you'll find the 3D digital technology of this master. I wonder if software creation can be divinely inspired. If it isn't, then developers are certainly using their God-engineered brain to design this spectacular technology. Either way God is glorified!

When you talk to most creators, whatever they did, they will say it just came naturally to them.

When you talk to most creators, whatever they did, they will say it just came naturally to them. They don't feel special; they put their pants on one leg at a time just like the rest of us. Think of Mozart as he was composing when he was only five years of age! It had to be natural for him; he heard it in his head and wrote it with his heart. God knew the gifts that Mozart possessed from the moment he was being formed in the womb—even before that! The musical beauty of this master is astounding. Did God want to demonstrate that life is bigger than the limits we have placed upon it? In Mozart, God used a *child* to change the world of music and to reflect His glory.

In life, we attempt to make sense of the world around us and we create small boxes of understanding. But God doesn't want us living in these boxes. Life is grand and through God's unmerited favor, He lets us experience His magnificence. God can use whomever He pleases.

In his book, *How To Think Like Leonardo da Vinci*,[2] Michael J. Gelb focuses on one of the world's most recognized geniuses. The entire world considers Da Vinci to be the epitome of the master. Some of Da Vinci's best known works include: the fresco painting of The Last Supper, the Mona Lisa, the Virgin of the Rocks and Madonna and Child. Da Vinci was also a renowned architect and sculptor. His understanding in the areas of

God wanted to demonstrate that life is bigger than the limits we have placed upon it. In Mozart, God used a *child* to change the world of music and to reflect His glory.

anatomy, botany, geology and physics were reflected in his studies, drawings and notes. He put many of these disciplines to use in his sketches of flight, helicopter, parachute, extendable ladder, armored tank, machinegun, mortar, guided missile and submarine, many of which are even used today. He pioneered automation, invented the three-speed gearshift, a thread cutting machine for screws, the bicycle, monkey wrench, snorkel, hydraulic jacks, waterwheel, folding furniture and more!

> The entire world considers Da Vinci to be the epitome of the master.

Gelb wanted to find commonalities such geniuses shared in their approach to life and learning. Listed below are the seven observation principals that Gelb discovered in his research:

Curiosita: An insatiably curious approach to life and an unrelenting quest for continued learning.

Dimostrazione: A commitment to test knowledge through experience, persistence and a willingness to learn from mistakes.

Sensazione: The continual reinforcement of the senses (especially sight) as the means to liven the experience.

Sfumato: Literally meaning going up in smoke. This refers to a willingness to embrace ambiguity, paradox and uncertainty.

Arte/Scienza: The development of the balance between science and art, logic and imagination; "whole-brain" thinking.

Corporalita: The cultivation of grace, ambidexterity, fitness and poise.

Connessione: The recognition of and appreciation for the interconnectedness of all things and phenomena; "systems thinking."

Gelb's book goes into more detail on each of these principals.[3]

The Holy Spirit helps us to ask the right "what if" and "why" questions.

> *I will ask the Father, and He will give you another Helper, that He may be with you forever;*
>
> John 14: 16

The Holy Spirit helps us to ask the right "what if" and "why" questions.

I would ascertain that we would all do well to carefully listen to the Holy Spirit's quiet whispers within. If we can drop the unchangeable past and focus on the unwritten future,[4] the breeding grounds of invention and discovery would be tilled.

Our sinful nature can negatively affect our ability to create.

Our sinful nature can negatively affect our ability to create.[5] There is evil running rampant, manifesting as greed, envy, lying, cheating, stealing, bearing false witness, lusting, adultery and the list goes on. Imagine life without these influences and tendencies. Picture God working with us in a sinless state. Imagine pure humanity, with clean countenance and conscience.[6] Without evil distractions, the creative process wouldn't be hindered.[7] We would be unencumbered masterpieces of God, more reflective of the image of *the* Master.[8]

Our approach to seeing God in the works of His people should open us to new revelations. God is about mystery. That is what makes life an adventure. These works don't have to be world-renowned to be legendary. The pursuit has to be instinctual, almost inhibition free; not caring about what anyone would be thinking of you in your pursuit, like a child grabbing for a prize! The last time I saw this look in a child's eyes is when I put on a dragon-training-themed birthday party for my son. I had rigged up a piñata-shaped dragon on a low-flying zip line and gave each child a turn with a wooden sword. The fight and determination I saw in their faces was remarkable. Each boy stepped forward, eyes bulging and tongues swirling, as they swung their swords to slay the dragon that was flying right into their faces. Their fears were conquered! Like these boys, I would like to be completely unencumbered and absolutely passionate in all my pursuits, including exploring the wonders of God and the mysteries of His creation. The boys became one with the their sword and their mission. A mission pre-wired in their DNA, which could swim around on the surface the size of a gnat's knee!

> I would like to be completely unencumbered and absolutely passionate in all my pursuits.

Richard Dawkins, the author of *The God Delusion*, is described as the world's most famous atheist and evolutionary biologist. Dawkins appeared at the Sheldonian Theatre in Oxford, England on February 23, 2012. His dialog shocked many listeners who attended the debate, which was titled, "The Nature of Human Beings and the Question of their Ultimate Origin." In spite of being a life-long proponent of maintaining a scientific perspective, Dawkins stated that he could in no way disprove God's existence. Based on that, Dawkins admitted that he could not be an atheist since he could not prove that God does not exist. This stance moves him into the realm agnosticism. Some may put Dawkins' early works in the "genius" category. One can be considered a genius and still change one's position regarding the existence of God. Here is a list of some famous scientists who believed in God:

1. Nicholas Copernicus (1473–1543)
2. Sir Francis Bacon (1561–1627)
3. Johannes Kepler (1571–1630)
4. Galileo Galilei (1564–1642)
5. Rene Descartes (1596–1650)
6. Isaac Newton (1642–1727)

7. Robert Boyle (1791–1867)
8. Michael Faraday (1791–1867)
9. Gregor Mendel (1822–1884)
10. William Thomson Kelvin (1824–1907)
11. Max Planck (1858–1947)
12. Albert Einstein (1879–1955)

Einstein and Isaac Newton made it to the top ten geniuses list as well. Einstein is probably the best known and most highly revered scientist of the twentieth century and is associated with major revelations in our thinking about time, gravity and the conversion of matter to energy ($E=mc^2$). Although never coming to belief in a personal God, he recognized the impossibility of a non-created universe. The *Encyclopedia Britannica* says of him: "Firmly denying atheism, Einstein expressed a belief in a. . . God who reveals himself in the harmony of what exists." This actually motivated his interest in science, as he once remarked to a young physicist: "I want to know how God created this world; I am not interested in this or that phenomenon, in the spectrum of this or that element. I want to know His thoughts—the rest are mere details." Einstein's famous epithet on the "uncertainty principle" was "God does not play dice"— and to him this was a real statement about a God in whom he believed. A famous saying of his was "Science without religion is lame, religion without science is blind."[9]

> However, one can be considered a genius and still change one's position regarding the existence of God.

Sir Isaac Newton was an English physicist, mathematician, astronomer, natural philosopher, alchemist and theologian, who has been "considered by many to be the greatest and most influential scientist who ever lived." Newton described universal gravitation and the three laws of motion, which dominated the scientific view of the physical universe for three centuries. Newton established standards for scientific publication still in use today.[10] Newton built the first practical reflecting telescope and developed a theory of color. He also formulated an empirical law of cooling and studied the speed of sound. In mathematics, Newton shares the credit with Gottfried Leibniz for the development of differential and integral calculus.[11] His list of great works goes on and on.

Which God-believing scientist will be next on the list?

Newton, although an unorthodox Christian, acknowledged God's hand in creation. Newton saw God as the masterful creator whose existence could not be denied in the face of the grandeur of all creation.[12]

Dr. William Lane Craig, theologian with a double doctorate, defender of historic Christianity, debated with Dr. Peter Atkins, the proclaimed atheist and renowned biologist. Dr. Craig stated that science cannot account for everything. He listed five things that cannot be scientifically proven: 1). Logic and mathematics; science presupposes logic and math, so trying to prove it by science would be arguing in circles. 2). Metaphysical truths. 3). Ethical statements of value. 4). Esthetic judgments. 5). Science itself cannot be justified because it's permeated with un-provable assumptions.

The idea that science cannot account for everything should come as a huge relief to scientists. Da Vinci learned the art of embracing that which is immeasurable. Piercing clarity would come out of the sciences if scientists would remain in the confines of what is measurable and include God as God in their equations. Professor Dr. Heribert Nilson, a botanist at Lund University in Sweden, concurs with this line of thinking. In his book, *Synthetische Artbildung* (The Synthetic Formation of Kinds), Nilson states, ". . . the theory of evolution is a severe obstacle for biological research. As many examples show, it actually prevents the drawing of logical conclusions from one set of experimental material, because everything must be bent to fit this speculative theory, an exact biology cannot develop."[13]

Dr. Peter Atkins stated that it would be "lazy" to give recognition to God and it is only bored and desperate people who need to believe in Jesus Christ. As Dr. Atkins fires his shots over the bow, I would suggest that his gifted mind of analysis is incapable of analyzing and considering God. Perhaps if he allowed the Spirit to bless him, he would be able to account for the immeasurable. Believers would do well to pray for unbelievers in the science community, for this is God's way of dismantling the work of the enemy. By the way, as uncomfortable as involvement in a spiritual battle may be, the strategic commander is also the one who abounds in grace and mercy. After the dust settles, He provides opportunities for everyone to choose a side. In this war, there is no draft or forced enlistment. The Creator's placement of free will in every member of the human race is of utmost importance and enlisting on the wrong side has dire, eternal consequences.

> The idea that science cannot account for everything should come as a huge relief to scientists.

> In this war, there is no draft or forced enlistment.

Seek and You Will Find

On March 12, 2012 a magnificent discovery was made. The long lost Da Vinci fresco titled "The Battle of Anghiari" was discovered on a wall, behind another wall depicting Giorgio Vasari's fresco titled "The Battle of Marciano." Da Vinci's masterpiece was discovered in the Plaza Veccio, Florence Italy's 14th century City Hall. However, to get to Da Vinci's piece, the works of Vasari had to be drilled through to the cavity where "The Battle of Anghiari" was hidden. With probes, experts were able

The Battle of Anghiari
Peter Paul Rubens' copy of "The Battle of Anghiari"

to carefully take samples. These samples have been analyzed with a scanning electron microscope. A black substance revealed an unusual chemical makeup of manganese and iron; this was the same black pigment compound found in brown glazes on Leonardo's "Mona Lisa" and "St John the Baptist." They have matched Da Vinci's fingerprints, as well as the layering techniques that are found in Da Vinci's work.

The researchers drilled in previously restored areas and fissures, not disturbing the original Vasari. They also took into consideration that Vasari was protecting Da Vinci's work. Whether right or wrong, they made the determination to reach one of the biggest finds in art history in decades. In time, perhaps the mystery behind the hiding of Da Vinci's work and its discovery will be revealed.[14] When we pursue God's truth, He tells us that we will find it. While examining the Vasari painting, a tiny flag was discovered. This flag does not appear to be connected to the scene. It reads: *Cerca trova.* This phrase is Italian for "Seek and you will find."[16] Some experts believe this to be a "note" left by Vasari to indicate the hidden work behind his own.

Like those who eagerly uncovered the work of this artistic master, God longs to reveal His Masterpieces. Through His Word and the divine moving of the Holy Spirit, the soul can be discovered. God uses the Holy Spirit, like the drills and probes used to reach DaVinci's masterpiece, to pierce the bone and marrow of our very being. Our pride, ego and even the lack of understanding are layers God has to drill through to get our attention.

> **God longs to reveal His Masterpieces!**

God's Word is described as a two-edged sword, piercing bone and marrow. What an incredible thought to ponder. In the words of Phillip Yancey, ". . . the universe was God's own work of Art, and the human body God's Masterpiece."[15] You and I are the Masterpieces of God!

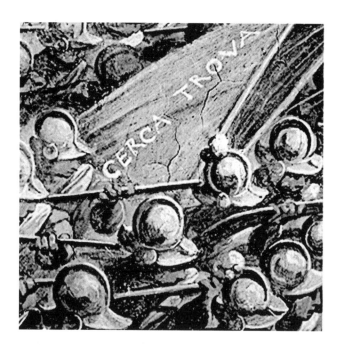

Cropping of the "Battle of Marciano" painting.

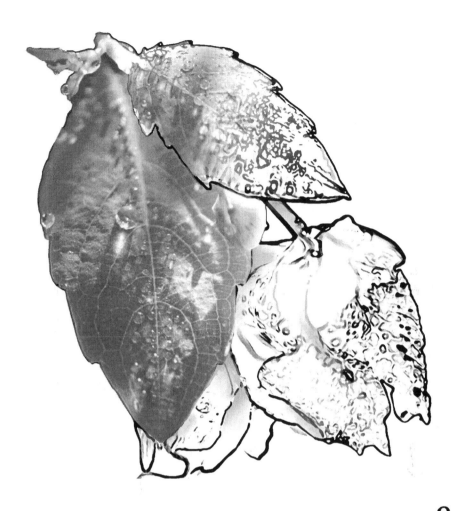

9
Unveiling Creation Design

God respects our free agency to choose—our free will. God is not jamming His authorship of everything that exists down our throats. He leaves our acceptance of the truth about creation in our own hands. He asks us to lean on faith rather than our own understanding. As the title of this chapter implies, there can be a veil shielding our view. At presentation ceremonies, there is an appropriate time to reveal whatever it is being featured. Presenters write an agenda of items that need to be addressed prior to unveiling. This adds drama and meaning to the event. Some items that may be covered prior to the unveiling include: the process, who did what, how long it took to create it, what sacrifices were made and the accolades of all involved. Next, as the veil drops and as the item is revealed, applause and delight follow. We do this because it's fitting for the occasion. I wonder if God is conducting a ceremony as His creation is unveiled to each of us. Perhaps as we began our walk with the Creator, we couldn't fully appreciate His handiwork because we were not able to see it. I have a missionary friend in Istanbul and this experience is very clear to her. When someone gets the big picture of faith, they begin to see beauty for the first time. Not that this is a soul barometer by any means, but an observation found in her area of ministry. Whatever the case, as we begin to see more and more, the appreciation of beauty and His handiwork are one of the rewards we get for seeking His Kingdom!

> He leaves our acceptance of the truth about creation in our own hands.

> I wonder if God is conducting a ceremony as His creation is unveiled to each of us.

Change Blindness

National Geographic examined an intriguing human behavior on one of their programs.[1] The camera crew created several situations, similar to the "Candid Camera" style of years gone by, to conduct some experiments. One scenario was done with a woman on a blind date. She was so focused on the male-female interaction that she was completely blind to the extensive activity going on around her. While the woman was engaged conversationally, the crew changed the entire restaurant—wall color, themes,

> When someone gets the big picture of faith, they can start to see beauty for the first time.

furniture and fabrics from a Chinese restaurant to a Mexican restaurant! She didn't see a thing! The term for this "limited view" is called *Change Blindness*. It refers to a blindness (or veiling) that occurs when our attention is focused so intently on one thing, that we neglect to notice everything else around us.

> Blindness (or veiling) occurs when our attention is focused so intently on one thing, that we neglect to notice everything else around us.

The National Geographic team set up another scenario with a hotel clerk registering hotel guests. Upon the arrival of each new guest, the crew had the hotel clerks swap themselves out with another clerk waiting below the counter. After a kind greeting to the hotel guest, the clerk went down under the counter to get something and then another clerk would come up and finish the task. None of the guests saw the new clerk because they were so focused on signing in. National Geographic conducted many similar scenarios demonstrating how veiling occurs when we are "hyper-focused." Few seem to be immune to this phenomenon.

I suggest that these same findings can be applied to our ability to see the things of God. The simple truths of understanding that can't be seen from one perspective can be revealed when our perspective changes. The Bible reminds us that, in Christ, all things become new. Sometimes this idea can encompass that which was once hidden and later becomes visible. Although we may begin to see the intangible truths, a narrow focus can inadvertently keep us from seeing the bigger picture that is being unveiled right before our eyes! The

> The enemy is highly skilled at the craft of distraction: Beware of his "slight of *mind*" deceptions.

enemy is highly skilled at the craft of distraction: Beware of his slight [*sleight* handwritten] of *mind* deceptions.

> The traps of the enemy are usually quite invisible and each one is set with a distinct motive in mind.

Enemy of Distraction

Almost as passionately as God pursues us, the enemy of God chases us, as well. Scripture teaches us Satan sets traps for us.

Then they will come to their senses and escape from the snare of the devil, who has taken them captive to his will.

II Timothy 2: 26 (BSB)

Not only is the enemy constantly setting snares for us, but the traps of the enemy are usually invisible and each one is set with a distinct motive in mind. The Bible teaches that the enemy who was struck down from heaven, roams the earth seeking whom to devour. Satan knows his time on earth is short and our time on this earth is about making a choice. If Satan can distract us long enough, he believes he can drag another soul with him into the realm of eternal suffering. If we can't see the handiwork of God in creation, the enemy is succeeding in distracting us.

I believe the devil is sardonically laughing at us because we are so easily distracted. Many can't get past the first commandment "thou shall have no other gods before Me." If these distractions take all of our time, and we are not pursuing God, we are losing the battle.

> A sad tragedy is that we can be distracted from pursuing our *own* story and the epic adventure yet to be written.

A sad tragedy is that we can be distracted from pursuing our *own* story and the epic adventure yet to be written! We wind up settling for watching other people's stories, factual or fictional. Sometimes our total social life revolves around what we'll see on TV next week. Moreover, as a nation, we seem especially interested in the "reality" shows about others. These shows depict dilemmas that we couldn't possibly imagine. We all have used distractions to pass the time or recuperate from a hard day at work or a challenging day taking care of our families. Our own lives can become so exhausting or unbearable that a distraction gets our minds off of our troubles for bit. . . before you know it, three hours have floated by, and we've been robbed of sleep, time with our family, or (more importantly) time we could have spent in God's presence.

Many people lose hours a day immersed in entertainment. Hollywood keeps cranking out epic dramas, which are not only entertaining, but have tremendous emotional appeal as well. We are strapped into a seat on a roller coaster ride that can thrill us beyond belief. It's quite a rush to experience great adventures without having to suffer any consequences or risk a thing—all for the price of admission!

Even today's authors will quote favorite movie scenes to help get a point across. It's so easy to do, especially when we have Hollywood investing millions in just a single action scene that communicates ideas so vividly. Why is so much energy being put into capturing our attention? Money of course! However, many writers, actors, producers and directors believe movies also offer meaning and purpose to the lives of their viewers.

On the flip side, some people feel that Hollywood is nothing but a pit of evil; the devil's playground, creating toxic thought and toxic thinking. Yes, when the content is destructive or meaningless, the enemy can enjoy lowering our morals, graying out what is right and wrong, encouraging the masses to become comfortable with sinful behavior and so on. Again, what's our response? Do we just sit and take it in, or do we take the time to communicate with our children about what the devil is truly doing here.[2]

Dr. Near'rot™ Zombie Doctor™

My wife and I, like many, use entertainment and our electronic devices as a reality escape. Yes, our life pains were mind numbing and unsolvable. The frustration levels, unbearable. So our escape quietly turned into an addiction. Why do I call it an addiction? Because it became a default, a pattern that the fruit of the time spent was zero—nada. It's embarrassing to write about, as the hours waisted are shameful. I didn't shake myself out of this. It was through an inspired dream that I realized my Zombie-like state. I share it with you in hopes it will assist you in making life-balance a priority.

The dreams that I recollect best are the ones that address a soul pain of sorts. This particular dream introduced me to a super hero like action figure. His packaging consisted of a large box with a see through window on the front. Inside was a plastic figure looking a little like Doc from the movie, *Back to the Future.* He had the wild hair, lab coat and even a stethoscope. When I read the packaging headline: *Dr. Near'rot™, Zombie Doctor™,* I laughed out loud and woke myself up!

> ...I was the one needing a Zombie Doctor.

I just had to figure the dream out. I ordered an action figure, clothes and even found a plastic head on ebay with wild white hair that I could modify. I came up with a logo, and made a visual prototype. So after all that, it occurred to me that I was the one needing Dr. Near'rot, Zombie Doctor. This is perhaps the best explanation of what happens to people becoming distracted by their entertainment and electronic devices.

God painstakingly inspired man to compose a Holy blueprint, a guide, a love letter that we can count on. When we are distracted and don't read the Bible, all we have is man's limited wisdom. We gather what we can in the eighty or so years we are given, but it just cannot be compared to the wisdom and omniscience of an eternal God.

Opening his mouth, Peter said: " I most certainly understand now that God is not one to show partiality.

Acts 10: 34–35

PC²

In a *60 Minute* segment about the life of Steve Jobs, co-founder of Apple, the question about his belief in God was raised. The biographer, Walter Isaacson, responded saying that Steve reflected his belief in the design of his devices. The words "on" and "off," and on-off switches are not found on any of his products. The biographer stated that Steve did this because he was hoping that there is an afterlife. Either Steve feared the nothingness of "off" or he didn't know his destiny well enough to offer a stance or a position. Maybe he felt that this information was simply none of our business. Even so, Steve will be remembered for his genius. After all, that's why we desired to know his perspective on life's biggest question. I know that if hell (a place of incredible torment) was my destiny after death, I would want to pursue my beliefs to a place of safety. I would certainly give the subject of afterlife some very serious thought. Did Steve hold a belief that when life is turned "off," or when one dies, that's it—lights out? Could someone as bright and intellectual as Steve Jobs truly believe there is nothing more? Perhaps. Anyone can be deceived, especially those that seem the brightest. Along with great intellect can often come great pride. Of course for the believer, our answer is a resounding "NO!" Beyond a shadow of a doubt, there is so much more. Through God, our story has meaning, purpose and most of all, we have *everlasting* life!

If we don't make up our minds regarding what we believe, the world may decide for us. It's so easy to just follow the crowd, to

> If we don't make up our minds regarding what we believe, the world may decide for us.

bend toward the trend of the day is. God is extremely clear that those who choose His way, the road less traveled, are a much smaller group than those who don't.

For the gate is small and the way is narrow that leads to life, and there are few who find it.

Matthew 7: 14

You will make known to me the path of life; In Your presence is fullness of joy; In Your right hand there are pleasures forever.

Psalms 16: 11

> "Jim, you have to accept that your perception of how narrow the road is, is not narrow enough."

After 3 hours of prayer and a day of fasting, I walked away discouraged as I didn't hear from the Lord as I expected. Then seconds later a very strong impression came. "Jim, you have to accept that your perception of how narrow the road is, is not narrow enough." I added this experience to this book as it just came to me three weeks prior to this writing. My wife and I have been sharing it and we are hearing that others have gotten a similar, "narrow is the road, message as well."

Distractions are keeping people off the narrow road. Satan is an expert at hiding the truth and using distractions to what's important. The enemy has over 5,000 years experience diverting man's attention away from God. He is the great thwarter and he will use every single resource he has to keep us from making a heart connection with God.

> The enemy has over 5,000 years experience diverting man's attention away from God.

In battle, there is something called a "war table." It's designed to help commanders see everything more objectively: the enemy's position, the lay of the land, the obstacles, the plan, the specific maneuvers and the intended goals of those involved. Part of the agenda may include knocking out communications. The first side to achieve this immediately increases their chances of getting the upper hand, if not a sure victory. Communication is vital and the enemy knows it. The same is true on the spiritual war front. If we can't hear from

> In our society, being "politically correct" can be interpreted in dangerous ways.

God, we are at risk of losing the most significant battle in the history of the world—one that has eternal consequences.

A popular mantra in corporate America encourages us to be "politically correct." This phrase is a stronghold in muzzling the messenger. In our society, being "politically correct" can be interpreted in dangerous ways. While we don't want to hurt anyone's feelings or be offensive in any way, when a message of hope can bring peace and life to someone, we should be able to provide that message to our fellow citizens. If the enemy is behind the use of this phrase, it has tremendous power. Hence, the name of this section, PC². (The "²" is used as a math multiplier. The initials "PC" means both Personal Computer and Politically Correct. Together, the story goes deeper than face value into areas of spiritual warfare.)

If indeed the enemy has a "war table," is there a small figurine with your name on it?. . . If so, what tactical distractive, deceptive or destructive maneuver is he employing?

> *Some people are like seed along the path, where the*
> *word is sown. As soon as they hear it, Satan comes*
> *and takes away the word that was sown in them.*
>
> Mark 4: 15 (NIV)

What Do You See Now?

I Corinthians 2 talks about the hidden and deeper things of God; those things which extend beyond natural or non-spiritual man's scrutiny. It's a spiritual matter to understand these deeper things that can only be given through the interpreter, the Holy Spirit. In verse ten, Paul points out that the Holy Spirit knows the heart of God and knows our heart too:

> **Paul points out that the Holy Spirit knows the heart of God and knows our heart too.**

Yet to us God has unveiled and revealed them by and through His Spirit, for the [Holy] Spirit searches diligently, exploring and examining everything, even sounding the profound and bottomless things of God.

I Corinthians 2: 10 (AMP)

> **So God teaches us to manage our thoughts.**

In one of Big Idea's *3-2-1 Penguins!* episodes called "The Carnival of Complaining", the host, Uncle Blobb asks a simple, yet profound question: "What do you see now?" Uncle Blobb reveals the positive and negative things that kids (and adults) often focus on. He demonstrates this while everyone is riding on a park monorail. The unpleasant host encourages them to see only the negative. Uncle Blobb spins everything negatively. He says that the ride "too old" or "too boring" or that it is "just for very little kids." As expected, this started a complaining spiral that would make any parent dizzy. So the fun rides just kept passing by the group and the children did not take the opportunity to enjoy themselves. In a similar way, opportunities in our own lives will keep passing us by. If we let long lines or the lack of cotton candy get us upset in the carnival of life, we can be left with a drained countenance. God teaches us to manage our thoughts. He does this because He knows that we can!

> *It is not what enters into the mouth that defiles the man, but what proceeds out of the mouth, this defiles the man.*

Matthew 15: 11

Opportunities in our own lives will keep passing us by if we focus on the negative.

At times I find myself behaving similar to these children. But, through the Holy Spirit, I can recognize or *see* the sinful behavior that I need to reject. The slight of mind tricks of the enemy go far beyond our desires for cotton candy. What do *you* "see" now?

Hardwired, Rooted In

What we see moves to our thought life. Dr. Caroline Leaf states: "Our own thoughts perform surgery on our brains with more precision than any neurosurgeon can. 75% to 95% of the illnesses that plague us today are a direct result of our thought life." Dr. Leaf is a cognitive neuroscientist with a PhD in Communication Pathology and a BSc in Logopedics and Audiology, specializing in metacognitive and cognitive neuropsychology.

> **"75% to 95% of the illnesses that plague us today are a direct result of our thought life."**
>
> Dr. Caroline Leaf, cognitive neuroscientist

 Dr. Leaf is currently raising awareness on What we think about affects us physically and emotionally. It's an epidemic of toxic emotions. Posted on her website November 25, 2018: https://drleaf.com/about/

toxic-thoughts/ is information on the havoc negative or toxic thoughts have on our bodies.

Once you begin to see truth, you are seeing things as God intended them to be seen. This is not as easy task as each veil can be considered a layer. E.g.: Youth are contending with faux norms— virtual living via games, esports, and a plethora of fantasy experiences. Who wouldn't want to take a light saber while donning virtual reality goggles, and joust with Darth Vader? If the time is not managed, these faux realities become dangerous safe places. And, as real social settings become more awkward, the "pretend offering" becomes more inviting.

> Once you begin to see truth, you are seeing things as God intended them to be seen.

As fast as we peel back the layers, new ones are coming into play fast and hard. This is where having a clear and balanced baseline for living is essential. Many in our culture are believing wrong is right and right is wrong. God knew this would happen:

"...Who substitute darkness for light and light for darkness;..."

Isaiah 5: 20

The Word of God is a reliable life baseline. The Word of God is life's filter. In the Lord's prayer it states, "Give us this day our daily bread." The Word is the bread of life and we are to take it in daily. The first Psalm tells us to "meditate on it day and night." The passage also reassures what will happen if we do this, "He is like a tree planted by streams of water, whatever he does, prospers." When our lives get uprooted via truth, getting replanted by living water will do great things.

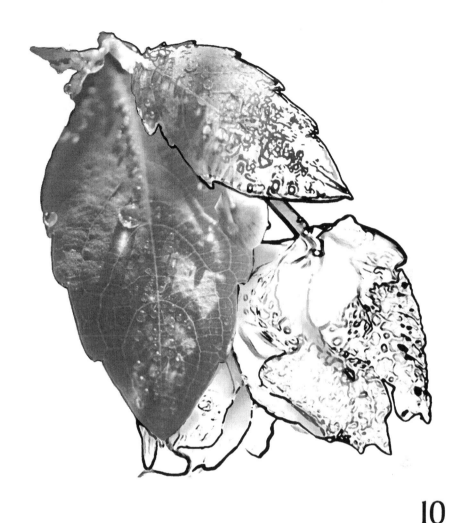

10

Obstacles That Keep Us from God's Passion

Unverified Information

This century has been dubbed the "information age." This brings blessings and responsibilities. The internet brings our lives into hyperspeed. We now have virtual interactions with one another and immediate access to an overwhelming plethora of information. This dynamic allows technology and innovation of every sort to enter an exponential state of growth. Within the realms of invention and discovery, this can be very good. However, it can also create a portal for errors and misinformation to spill into our laps. Unfortunately, it is impossible to fully process the huge volume of information coming to us, literally, at the speed of light.

One of the necessary checks and balances we need to incorporate into our filtering process is common, intelligent and intentional scrutiny. Information in and of itself has power and we are wise to be careful with that power. Misuse of technology can make, break or even destroy individuals, marriages and corporations. Even the government is not immune to the havoc that can result from the right information in the wrong hands. It can positively or negatively affect what will happen to people with their jobs, reputation, property and a host of other areas. Misinformation can misdirect and confuse while good information can have unlimited positive influence in our lives.

> Misuse of technology can make, break, or even destroy individuals, marriages, and corporations.

> Misinformation can misdirect and confuse.

One example of this is in our media today. You have heard the term "Fake News." Mass media is currently being challenged for serving one side of a two party system. In the past, the news presented the concerns, agendas, and plans of both sides objectively. Currently, two media giants are being sued by a high school student for defamation of character. The combined dollar amount is $525 million.

It is of the utmost importance that we possess true integrity in our day-to-day living. If we are presenting information, we are to make every effort to be as error-free as possible. As human beings, we all have some element of bias. However, we must force ourselves to have an objective eye. We need to stop the information process "rocket ride" and take time to evaluate and triple check our sources. When we do, the process of setting aside unverified data or unproven hypotheses begins. Once this is done, it will help us to see creation and truth in its purest sense, as God intended things to be. Pursuing truth will also help us to navigate through what is false.

Be still, and know that I am God. . .

Psalms 46: 10 (NKJV)

Leaving God Out

Science is one area easily affected by new technological advances, discoveries and theories. Some of these assumptions have been helpful in developing new theories, while others have been spun into old distorted scientific paradigms (sets of philosophical or theoretical frameworks). If years go by without acknowledging new discoveries that don't fit the paradigm, the scientific community and the world lose. They lose not only important information that could shed light on current and past research, but even more importantly, God is ignored, belittled and not given the glory due Him. The latter is the most dangerous.

> Today's findings can be in conflict with yesterday's assumptions.

Some evolutionary samples of the earth and creation origins, alternatives to biblical creationism may include these ideologies:

- ". . . mystical tinkering mechanism that miraculously spits out new . . ."[1]
- ". . . intelligence [other than God, such as aliens] must be involved for the extraordinarily diverse elements to work together.[1]
- The passing of time created. . .
- An epic explosion created. . .
- Need in and of itself creates. . .

Our quest for discovery should not ignore the hand of deity. If we are ignoring God's hand in creation, it would be good to search our hearts and ask ourselves why? Is there really a good enough reason? If there is a fear in recognizing God, then those fears should be addressed one at a time. Some of these fears may include:

- Recognizing God will be a hindrance or crutch in my discovery.
- If I recognize God, I will have to be accountable for what's right and wrong.
- If I recognize God, my peers will look down on me.
- If I recognize God, I will get lazy about going the extra mile.
- If I recognize God, it may jeopardize my job.
- If I recognize God, I may have to change my belief system.
- If I recognize God, I may have to eat a slice of humble pie.

> When the essence of science is *true discovery*, our fears shouldn't hinder us.

When the essence of science is *true discovery*, our fears shouldn't hinder us. Like many fields of study, the discipline to go further—to go deeper in understanding shouldn't be at all mired! The popular politically correct excuse for leaving God as the Creator out of the discussion is that it "isn't scientific." The real reason is that it would call for some kind of accountability on our part. The intersection between science and religion, regarding the origin of life, needs to look at all plausible theories, rather than exclude the ones that don't align with their worldview.

[handwritten margin note:] RIGHT

[handwritten margin note:] WRONG

> God doesn't need human validation.

The Bible teaches that we are *made* to glorify God, *not* to take the glory away.

This information intersection (between science and religion) regarding the origin of life needs to *include* information, rather than exclude it. That means *all* information validated by both history and geology should be part of the discussion. Although God does not need validation; archeology, geology, and history have confirmed much of the Word of God and its' written accounts.

> Fields of study which touch upon life's origin should at least include the *plausibility* that "God created."

Paul Garner brings interesting facts to life regarding this topic in the introduction of his book, *The New Creationism*. He states, "Major disciplines of science were founded by men of Christian convictions, such as Boyle, Ray, Hooke, Newton, and Faraday. These giants were motivated by their spiritual beliefs! Like the astronomer Kepler, they perceived that in their scientific insights they were 'thinking God's thoughts after him'. Today, there is an embarrassed silence and a collective amnesia about the religious motivations of these men. This disconnect from biblical roots is atheistic in practice."[3]

Garner's sentiments clearly establish a tremendous obstacle which prevents many of God's children from seeing the intense love and passion that the great Designer has in His heart for each of us.

> God is omniscient and is watching! His ways provide a benchmark that is reliable. If we drift from this, then whose benchmark do we use? Drifting has a price.

Fields of study which touch upon life's origin should at least include the *plausibility* that God created. Would the infamous Solyndra event (500 million dollars invested by our government in a solar panel industry that failed) ever have happened if good science and/or thorough market research were initially presented? Were our leaders who invested this money on the public's behalf initially misled? Or, were regulatory or policy uncertainties the cause? Not to pick on just Solyndra, but GE put a halt on their energy project in this area as well. The point here is **not** to enter a blame game, but to make every attempt to include complete truth in all that we do. God is omniscient and is watching! His ways provide a benchmark that is reliable. If we drift from this, then whose benchmark do we use? Drifting has a price. It can be costly and keep us from true discovery. Garner was not alone in his ideas. Our nation's foundational laws are based on biblical principals. Three examples that are biblical: Thou shall not murder, steal or bear false witness (slander). We don't want to continue losing sight of evidence that doesn't fit into the current "PC" model. According to Dr. Heribert Nilson, "the theory of evolution is a severe obstacle for biological research. As many examples show, it actually prevents the drawing of logical conclusions from one set of experimental material. Because everything must be bent to fit this speculative theory, an exact biology cannot develop."[4] Observable evidence must always take precedence over theoretical assumptions.

This God-Created concept helps us avoid basing our findings on commonly held assumptions in science. As these assumptions are proven wrong by today's observable evidence, it leaves society in a quagmire of misinformed muck.

Today's research and findings can affect the populous in ways beyond our human understandings. Acknowledging our Creator is the only choice. It opens the opportunity to broaden our understanding and see things on a much deeper level.

This God-created concept helps us avoid basing our findings on commonly held assumptions in science. As these assumptions are proven wrong by today's observable evidence, it leaves society in a quagmire of misinformed muck. Once again we are prevented from seeing and experiencing God's passion for us.

The American evangelist, Billy Graham, made a relevant statement regarding education: "America's founding fathers did not intend to take religion out of education. Many of the nation's greatest universities were founded by evangelists and religious leaders; but many of these have lost the founders' concept and become secular institutions. Because of this attitude, secular education is stumbling and floundering." Evidence of this is found in the surge of private school openings. This is something we should not stick our heads in the sand about.

> Complex genetic information in the form of genes and regulatory DNA *cannot* randomly evolve.
>
> Jeffrey Tomkins, Ph.D.,
> *Institute for*
> *Creation Research*

Societal Misconceptions

To help simplify things, the terms "good science" and "bad science" will be used in this section of the book. Good science consists of witnessed, observable evidence without assumptions. Bad science is just the opposite—no witnesses, no observable evidence and it is loaded with assumptions.

Assumptions can be derived from:

- Theories that are based on generalizations, with a deductive (limited knowledge base) structure.
- Elegant consistencies within a synthetic (man-made) universe. Models are not reality, no matter how elegant.
- The assertion of the consequent: A model or set of equations has a finite (limited) domain of validity.
- One-sided, 'peer reviewed' content published in journals.
- Ossification (to become set in a rigidly conventional pattern, a paradigm which is a philosophical or theoretical framework of any kind) of current assumptions.[5]

Scientific submissions regarding assumptions about creation would have a tough time holding up in today's court of law. They would, however, be accepted and published as **fact** should a *single peer* within a *peer review*, review it.[6] There is more information and a solution in the Addendum of this book. *No peer reviews are conducted by*

As scientists continue to learn more and more about the genetic *a single peer!*

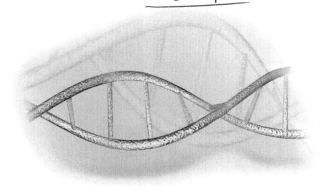

makeup of living things, it becomes increasingly difficult for them to fit their discoveries into the evolutionary model. In fact, these new discoveries actually negate evolutionary theory. A recently published discovery in the prestigious British journal *Nature*, proves such a point by stating that complex genetic information in the form of genes and regulatory DNA *cannot* randomly evolve.[7] *Replacing Darwin* by Nathaniel T. Jeanson, goes into great detail regarding trait origins, genes and many recent discoveries made in the molecular.

Below are a few of the "proven" theories that have been refuted by recent observable evidence. To read more about these and other refuted theories, view "The Riddle of Origins Series", a DVD series by Mike Riddle, produced by *Answers In Genesis*.[8]

NOTE / Warning: This is a highly controversial area. Obviously, there are no eyewitnesses that can truly verify young or old earth origins. My hope is that God's Word will not be overshadowed by this or any other area of the creation mystery. God uses the mysteries of life for His greater and transcendent purposes.

B.S.

- Were millions of years needed for fossil and coal development? Observable evidence found at Mt. St. Helen's refutes this by demonstrating that it only took two weeks for fossils and 20 years for coal.
- How about the millions of years needed for canyon development? Observable evidence found at Mt. St. Helen's refutes this as well, it only took five days.
- What about the animal species identified as extinct millions of years ago? Observable evidence of living "fossils" found without any evolutionary transformation such as the Coelacanth fish and Selakant.

> New observable evidence should make evolutionary theories open for redefinition today.

- Did the human race evolve from primordial ooze? The failed Miller experiment produced the wrong enzyme needed for spontaneous life.
- Is the earth 4.54 billion years old? Modern observable data from the moon encourages views of a much younger earth.
- Did we evolve from monkeys? Archeological audits of Neanderthal man, Piltdown man, Lucy, etc. revealed that the skeletal findings were either falsified or grossly misrepresented on dig locations. Bone segments were often found in bone "graveyards" miles and even years apart and then put together to form one specimen. *Who says we were ever monkeys?*

"Einstein's relativity, teaches that time, space, and light were not what we thought them to be. After relativity emerged, all of physics—even all of reality—was open for redefinition.[9]" In the same way, new observable evidence should make evolutionary theories open for redefinition today.

The observable evidence easily moves biblical creation claims to a plausible status.

If the first 13 verses of Genesis are false, then what does that say about the rest of the Bible?

We demolish arguments and every pretension that sets itself against the knowledge of God, and we take captive every thought to make it obedient to Christ.

II Cor. 10:5 (NIV)

Many are concerned about leaving God out of the science picture. Hence, one of the reasons for home school popularity.

Denying the existence of a creator (which is the foundation of Genesis teaching), leads one to begin to question if the whole Bible can be trusted. If the first 13 verses of Genesis are false, then what does that say about the rest of the Bible? Once again, when we deny the Creator, we also turn our backs on His incredible boundless love for us, and reject the remarkable journey He has in store for us in this life—and the next!

Ken Ham, founder of Answers In Genesis (AiG-USA), and Ark Encounter KY states: "Compromising Genesis has contributed toward the loss of biblical authority in our nation and helped open the door to the secularization of the culture."[10]

The Bible states that it is the Word of God, written by holy men of God. According to John, "In the beginning was the Word and Word was with God and is God." Genesis says that it took God six days to create *everything*. When we doubt this, we set into motion a cascade of disbelief in, not only the miracles of God, but biblical authority as well.

> It would stand to reason that we would be open to new and astounding conclusions in that discovery process.

I suppose it all boils down to believing the Bible in a literal or figurative sense. One biblical concept that many argue about is in 2 Peter 3:8, "But do not overlook this one fact, beloved, that with the Lord one day is as a thousand years and a thousand years as one day." Studying the original text and the context of this verse and the words "day" and "years" are paramount to understanding the meaning behind it. I believe in a literal six-day creation. I do not have time to expound on this here, so please spend some time asking God for clarity as you search out the truth of the meaning of these verses. One very plausible explanation of the meaning of these verses can be found in "The Berisheet Prophesy."[11] Spend some time researching the evidence of a young earth and God's creation by looking at some of these resources: Answers In Genesis (AiG-USA), Institute for Creation Research (ICR), Creation Ministries International (CMI), Reasons To Believe, Biblical Creation Society, Creation Biology Study Group, Geoscience Research Institute, Creation Research Society, Earth History Research Center, WorldView Ministries, Creation Research UK, Creation Resources Trust, Creation Science Movement, Truth in Science and Creation Today. These offer hundreds of titles on biblical creation. And the interest on the subject is rising! Many are concerned about leaving God

> The "Genesis account," fits many of the missing pieces together.

out of the science picture. Hence, one of the reasons for the rise in home school popularity.

Most people today like to be intellectually engaged. Our civilization is making extraordinary advances on all fronts by using the latest equipment and technology. It would stand to reason that we would be open to new and astounding conclusions in that discovery process.

What encouraged science of past history to leave out flat earth findings in the textbooks of yesterday?

As we discover new molecular evidence that upends the foundation of evolutionary theory, many scientists are scrambling to find a new model in which to fit this evidence. Acknowledging God's role in creation forms a framework for this new information. The molecular data points to intelligent design….by a loving God. Secular science does all it can to shut down the spread of this discovery of order, design, and purpose in the molecular. Because, if this is true, we must answer to someone or something bigger than ourselves. Evolution gives mankind the power to deny the Creator, His power *and* authority.

In the short 200+ years of America's existence, God advanced the progress of mankind like never seen before.

This country was founded on Judeo-Christian principals. They never fail. In the short 200+ years of America's existence, God advanced the progress of mankind like never seen before.

We drift toward failure in our attempts to be "people pleasers vs. God pleasers."

Why did past scientists drop the flat earth theory for a new one? Observable evidence changed their minds. Why do we try and fit new biological and technological advances into a model developed in 1859? We are well beyond this path. This model is based on a theory developed before our discovery of DNA[12] and our invention of the electron and atomic microscope. The discoveries that we are making today are

believe. It's back, too! Since everyone believes what they want iregardless of facts

Why do we try and fit new biological and technological advances into a model developed in 1859?

not only known by our Creator, but He is the Originator of these as well! To acknowledge God as Creator takes us all the way back to the beginning and gives us hope for the future.

If the secular scientific community does not adjust itself and begin to apply all new, proven, or observable evidence to their scientific research models—even if it does not fit into their existing models—then we, as a society have a responsibility to ask why. The most likely answer to the above question is fear. There is a fear of ridicule, fear of not being taken seriously, or fear of losing their position or standing within the scientific community. We are not to worry about what others may think of us. The Bible is clear on this, "... speak, not as pleasing men, but God who examines our hearts." I Thes. 2:4. When I run into a scientist or science instructor that recognizes God as their creator, I am reminded of the career risk they are taking and I esteem them greatly for their bravery and objectivity.

In his book *Ignorance: How it Drives Science*, Dr. Stuart Firestein, doesn't mince words on this topic: "What makes a scientist is ignorance. This may sound ridiculous, but for scientists, the facts are just a starting place." Dr. Firestein's point holds true as the sea of new information creates oceans of questions. He continues by saying that, ". . . thoroughly conscious ignorance. . . is a prelude to every real advance in knowledge."[13]

Scientists work very hard to be accepted into acclaimed schools. They pay for a high quality education and expect to receive high quality information. These individuals are using

Evolution give's mankind the power to deny the Creator, His power *and* authority.

their gifts of knowledge to make scientific observations. In many cases, they didn't grow up with any sort of Bible teaching in the home, so there could have simply been a void of knowledge in biblical matters. If a scientist would take the time to gain understanding, his or her world would expand beyond the human constraints of known knowledge.

We contribute to the secularization of our nation when we dismiss God as irrelevant to science. The church has played a significant role by being relevant. The book *Already Gone* by Ken Ham and Britt Beemer (written with Todd Hillard) presents revealing research statistics that deserve attention.[14] The book illustrates a strong symbolic sample of the short road to irrelevance. Charles Darwin popularized a philosophy that hit at the very foundation of the church (the Word of God). Surprisingly, Darwin was honored by the church and is even buried in the foundation of Westminster Abby. *Already Gone*, although focused on a smaller window of research, offers several ways that the church could be more relevant in today's world. We all have quite of bit of yielding to do in regard to what we find as real truth. It is always good to bear in mind how God is working globally and, guess what? God's people are indeed winning![15]

Religious leaders of the day imprisoned Galileo for his discoveries, but later learned through scientific discovery that Galileo was right. Maybe the church leaders were thinking. . . *We don't want to blow this one. Let's bury Darwin here as a public statement in our support of science.* It seems that Darwinism, evolution and millions of years, ironically, got buried in our children's brains as well.

We are called by God to seek out wisdom, knowledge, and truth. To understand the things of God is not a field of study per se, but a journey of personal faith. God defines our journey by pointing out that as children, we subsist on milk (that which is easy to grasp), but as we mature we need solid food (understanding that will take more study). In most of life's pursuits, being teachable is a required attribute.

Science is a contributor to many good things in life. It should never be taken for granted. Here is a very small snapshot of areas where science has been extremely influential:

- Helping with cures for diseases and improved health
- Gene therapy to restore meaningful vision to people with LCA and other forms of inherited blindness
- Chochlear implants provide a sense of sound
- Forensic sciences, investigation, DNA, engineering, psychology, drug chemistry
- Technologies to protect lives and livelihood from the effects of earthquakes, volcanic eruption, floods
- Reliable water for sustainable development
- Providing a basis for restoration of ecosystems throughout the country and world
- Innovations to improve industry and technology
- Energy and natural resource exploration

We are definitely grateful for the men and women who are making great strides in the field of science. However, the crucial issues of life should cause us to be prudent on how we evaluate the scientific interpretation of the world around us. Tough questions to ask ourselves are: "In research, which viewpoint should my observations come from? A worldview or a biblical creation view? Which would be reasonable in guiding me?" "Will this perspective influence my decisions?" "Are there others to seek out for support and brain storming?" "How can I nurture this idea to my peers?" "What happens if I lose my funding, if so, are there other funding sources to approach?" These are not easy questions for anyone. Although the cost is high when it comes to making claims in the scientific world, it's also high if we sacrifice our personal faith. We have a responsibility to be careful with issues that can affect outcomes, not only in this world, but also in the one to follow.

Standing up for what's right and true can be costly. I know because it made our life very difficult. We lost well into the six digits for standing up for our beliefs. It put some areas of our life into a tormenting downward spiral. However, I can now say that there were life lessons that I needed to learn and this was a sure way to get my attention.

Another societal misconception is that all scientists hold to evolution as fact. The *Select List of Science Academics, Scientists, and Scholars Who are Skeptical of Darwinism* was compiled by Jerry Bergman PhD. This group is large, consisting of some 3,000 Darwin skeptics. And it is quite extensive. This study can be obtained at https://www.rae.org/essay-links/darwinskeptics/.[16]

> Over 1.9 Billion logged-in users visit YouTube each month and every day people watch over a billion hours of video and generate billions of views.
>
> YouTube "Statistics"
> Accessed November 26, 2018

There is an additional list of 1,000 names which are unpublished. Dr. Bergman is honoring their request to not make their name public. Another list, from Dissentfromdarwin.org[17] tallies over 1070. Because verification of the information on lists such as these can be difficult and time consuming, they are not created often. However, the data that is available is interesting, to say the least.

Our Own Thinking. . . and Barriers to Learning

Communication is not complete if the intended message never reaches its destination. Whether its verified or unverified information, for God or against God, it's useless if it's not received and processed. William D. Winn, Director of the Learning Center, Human Interface Technology Laboratory at the University of Washington Educators states, "Children raised with the computer—think differently from the rest of us. They develop hypertext minds. They leap around. It's as

> **Communication is not complete if the intended message never reaches its destination.**

though their cognitive structures were parallel, not sequential." Peter Moore expounds on this point in an Inferential Focus briefing by saying, "Linear thought processes that dominate educational systems now can actually retard learning for brains developed through game and Web-surfing processes on the computer."[18] In other words, the old way of learning just got older and is not a relevant learning style.

Today we are taking in information differently. As of 2018, YouTube stats include:

- Over 1.9 billion logged in users visit YouTube each month
- Over a billion hours of video are watched everyday on YouTube
- Facebook had 2.27 billion monthly active users[19]
- U.S. Twitter users amounted to 67 million in 3rd qtr. 2018[20]

However, what does it take to get information into the part of the brain for it to be useful? Are digital devices and entertainment the distraction of today? Two distinct people groups have emerged from our digital age. One group represents those that are life spectators and the other group, although much smaller in size, are life's participants. The spectators are just that: *watchers* of life. It seems as though when life calls for basic initiative engagement, there's a disconnect and the message isn't reaching the part of the brain for application. The critical thinking part of the brain can have an "unconscious-like" tendency. This can encourage a

> **Two distinct people groups have emerged... life spectators and life participants.**

"do nothing" response. Basic initiatives to engage safety or offer help is not likely to enter the picture with the spectator group. What were the distractions 2,000 years ago? Certainly not a drop-down movie player from the second hump of a camel! They surely were not obsessed with games like *Fortnite* or *Minecraft but they were obsessed with idols* of their day. They also had trouble with obeying God, the misuse of power and money, and whom or what they worshipped. This is one of the reasons why Jesus came to earth—Jesus addressed the condition of the heart and the sinful nature of man. It would be safe to say that we haven't evolved much in 2,000 years!

> Not "still" as a couch potato, but resting in His control of life's details...

Think about all the faces which are glowing in the soft, bluish light of the LCD screens. People stare at their screens for hours, often missing opportunities to love each other, to reach out to others, or just to meditate on what God has done. God asks us to "Be still and know that I am God." Not "still" as a couch potato, but resting in His control of life's details. God says, "Draw near to Me and I will draw near to you." God warns that He will reject us if we have not built a relationship with Him. God is talking to busy believers with mixed-up priorities. God defines two types of people: those that know Him, and those that don't. If our life priorities are off track, not having a handle on the first commandment, we have very little time for seeing or experiencing God.

> The rise of the digital generation has also created two people groups, the digital native and the digital immigrant.

The rise of the digital generation has also created two people groups, the digital native and the digital immigrant. Those born into the digital age have the advantage of actually being wired to this new form of information and learning; the digital immigrants have to work hard to develop these new pathways to learning this through study and experience. Teachers must now compete with the fast-paced information stream that comes at these students at every given moment. There is a constant pressure to make the information more entertaining and easier to grasp for these young "digital natives".

Dr. David A. Sousa, an international educational consultant and author of *How the Brain Learns*, states that some children who are currently labeled "learning disabled" may be more accurately described as "schooling disabled." Sousa adds that, "Sometimes, these students are struggling to learn in an environment that is inadvertently designed to frustrate their efforts. Just changing our instructional approach may be enough to move these students to the ranks of successful learners."

> There seems to be constant pressure to make the information easier to grasp for the young "digital natives."

Teachers of biblical concepts would do well to do the same. It could be fun! Incorporating visual creativity into Bible presentations is a great way to engage these "digital natives". By including the creative and biblical arts in your teaching, you can really help communicate the best message on the planet! A real help to instructors is given in the next chapter as a generational transformer. They offer free, dramatic and colorful animations in high resolution on hundreds of biblical topics.

Whether its a falsehood, a fantasy or an out-of-date teaching style it's good to have a clear understanding of the obstacles that keep us from reaching our objectives.

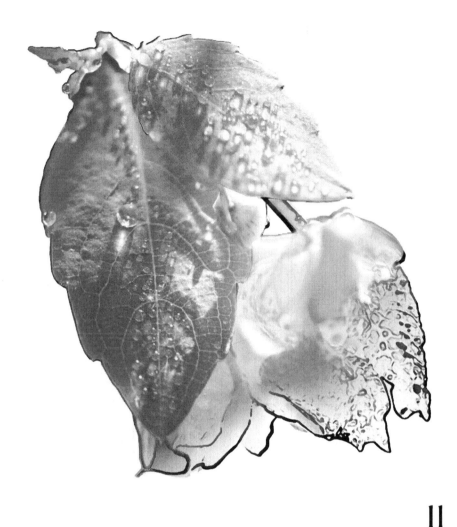

11
Transformers

People tend to resist change. Good or bad, change can be difficult. Good changes such as starting your dream job or the arrival of that baby you've wanted for so long, can be both exhilarating and terrifying. On the other hand, change that involves loss can be doubly difficult, even devastating. Death, separation from a loved one, changes in health, loss of a job, home, or any disruption in the status quo can have tremendous impact on our faith and outlook. Change affects all of us, all the time. It's not a matter of *if,* it's a matter of *when* change will affect us.[1] Facing it head-on can be difficult. In fact, many of us refuse to do so. We easily find ways to practice avoidance. It's only natural!

In the movie *Transformers,* the producers, directors and designers go over the top in creating transformations. The 3D software technology, creativity and immense amount of patience it took, combine to make these highly detailed transitions possible. The cars, trucks and newly invented beasts, literally turn themselves inside out several times (in explicit and exaggerated detail) as they reconfigure into a new shape. You see the inner stainless steel mechanics, gears, hydraulics, cylinders, cables, bearings, connectors and pulleys—and that's just what is recognizable! The movie is based on Hasbro's Transformer toys.

> Change affects all of us all the time. It's not a matter of *if;* it's a matter of *when* change will affect us.

However, theses transformers are not toys. The figures convert to Godzilla-sized, armed and armored, jet-packed robots. Your mind cannot grasp the amount of detail that unfolds right before your eyes! The computer-generated graphics are very realistic. It's hard not to buy into this virtual reality *as* reality! All the radically moving parts end up tucking neatly together in each final transition. According to *Animation World Network,* it took 38 hours for ILM (Industrial Light and Magic) to render just one frame of movement in this movie.

You know what you're seeing on the silver screen isn't real, but you buy into it anyway. The changes we witness on screen do not carry any tragic impact for us, unlike real life. It's great escapism! Seldom do we have a way to escape from the changes life brings. Our instinctive fear of the unknown can paralyze us and keep us from experiencing the great adventures that God has in store for us.

God created the concept of change before the beginning. God scripted changes throughout the silver screen of life. He knows our insecure state. God left us His Word and His universe. Since we are creatures of habit, God gave us some stable markers throughout His creation. He gave us the sun that continues to burn brightly and the seasons that come and go every year. He gave us changes that we can depend on. They comfort us by letting us know that there is order in the universe. The world keeps turning and God is on His throne. Yet, He is still a God of unexpected change.[2] These powerful reminders are the transformers of our reality that help us keep our attention centered on Him.

God even uses His creatures to teach this. For example, the butterfly is the epitome of a transformed life. It turns from the lowly, almost awkward caterpillar to a beautiful winged-wonder. The caterpillar magically turns into a chrysalis, its body becoming a puddle of goo, and emerges as something quite unrelated to its humble beginnings! These creatures seem to embrace change with unmatched beauty and grace. This is what the Father desires for us! He wants to transform us from our humble beginnings to the image of Christ! Ahhh, and what joy we bring Him if we do it with the grace of the butterfly!

Change is a necessity for life-sustaining order. There are many useful things that He designed to spring forth from decay, like coal, mulch and fertilizer. The processes of evaporation in the ever-changing hydrological cycle includes changes in the state of water, from vapor, to liquid, to ice.[3]

God says that we are to change, physically, mentally and spiritually. After our bodies expire, we change residence.[4] As creatures with curiosity, we gather as much knowledge as possible to help us through life. After all, knowledge is power! And through that knowledge, we grow in our relationship with God.

The opportunity to grow spiritually is the breath-taking element. It's

> These powerful reminders are the transformers of our reality that help us to keep our attention centered on Him.

truly vital in our adventure on this planet. If we throw ourselves completely into this venture, trusting completely in all that our Creator has
in store for us without fearing the unknown, life (and beyond) would
become so much more than we ever imagined it could be!

The Bible tells us that by the renewing of our minds, all things become new. This is a power-packed verse, to say the least. "Old things
have passed away; behold, all things have become new," 2 Corinthians
5: 17 (NKJV)) is a great promise. The Bible also tells us that God will
restore the years the locust has eaten, "Then I will make up to you for
the years That the swarming locust has eaten," Joel 2: 25. God promises
to restore us from sinful, selfish creatures to images of Christ. With a
new mind, we get new perspective. This new perspective can give us
hope for the future, even in pressing situations. Our new mind begins
to reflect the mind of Christ. It gives us the insight and knowledge to change our circumstances. If we can have the mind of Christ,
we begin to see things through His eyes, and understand the lessons
He wants to teach us and the path He wants us to take. We will begin
to really grasp the power of prayer when what seemed immovable, is

> Are we willing to risk it all as a demonstration of our desired friend-ship with God?

suddenly moving!

In another verse, God communicates that our spiritual growth
begins with "milk." This milk is a metaphor for easy-to-understand
principals and promises of God. We are not to stay on milk forever.
Just as a baby is weaned from milk to solid food, so we too should
mature to "solid food." How do we do this? By studying the Word
of God for the deeper and richer things of God. This 'milk-to-meat'
change is how God designed our spiritual walk. We are to grow in the
admonition of the Lord.

If we are parents, we manage our children's metamorphosis by
bringing them up in the way that they should go. What about those

decisions that we know they have to make that may result in painful changes? Sometimes making those changes seems impossible. They may have serious repercussions if they make the wrong choice. We must let them forge ahead, because God is bigger than all of us and He is in charge.

God is patient and not bound by time. He is in no hurry, but we are. We want the answers now! We want God to work in OUR time frame! We need to be patient and trust God to give us direction. We need to remember to surrender our thoughts and desires to Him. We are to pray for wisdom and God says that He will grant us it[5] He also tells us that there is wisdom in the counsel of many. One of the things that I like to do to help me get a clearer perspective on a decision is to write a list of pros and cons. I try to define all the possibilities of a decision that requires change. I include not only myself in the equation, but also how my decision might affect others.

I take comfort in knowing my decisions are spiritually based. In addition, Jesus words, "If you confess me before others, I will confess you before the Father" bring me solace. This, I believe is the ultimate crisis of life. Am I willing to risk it all as a demonstration of my desire for friendship with God? God willingly gives me the free gift of eternal life—complete with heir status as a child of the King! Why wouldn't I?

Lee Strobel is a former atheist, lawyer and investigative reporter who realized he had to investigate the claims of Christianity, rather than blindly accept or reject what he was taught. After almost two years of intensive investigation, he concluded that the evidence overwhelmingly supported the claims of Christianity. When Lee and his wife were married, she was an agnostic and he was an atheist. Later, when Lee's wife made the decision to follow Jesus Christ, it made Lee uncomfortable. He saw a change in her character that was both winsome and attractive. He went to church with other motives, thinking perhaps that she was in a cult. He heard the message of Jesus Christ articulated in an understandable way. From there, Lee used his skills as an investigative reporter and went about investigating the claims of the Bible for nearly two years. The evidence that he gathered was so overwhelming that he realized *it would take more faith* for him to continue as an atheist than to become a believer in Jesus Christ![6]

As an agnostic college student, **Josh McDowell** believed that Christianity was worthless. But a group of Christians challenged him to examine the claims of Christianity on an intellectual basis. Instead of succeeding in discrediting the truth of Christianity, Josh discovered compelling historical evidence for the reliability of the Christian faith. As a result, Josh accepted Christ as his personal Savior and Lord, and he found his life changed through God's love and grace.[7]

Antony Flew was a contemporary British philosopher who was quite notorious throughout the world for his atheistic views (even referencing himself as such in one of his own book titles). Flew's arguments against God included: 1. The universe is eternal. 2. Life is a random process. 3. God is a self-contradiction. The academic world was set on its ear when, after much consideration, he converted to deism. He stated in an interview that the advancements of science itself reveal the integrated complexity of the physical world. Flew saw intelligence in the manifestation of life written in DNA, the transcription of DNA to RNA, RNA into proteins and the subsequent process of protein folding. . . He realized that intelligence *must* be involved for the extraordinarily diverse elements to all work together in harmony. Consciousness and reproduction considerations were influential in his subsequent conversion to theism as well. Rest in peace, Antony Flew.[8]

> God states that He disciplines those he loves.

These gentlemen all have exhibited faith by letting go of man's understanding and resting in their Creator's words.

Trust in the Lord with all your heart and lean not on your own understanding; in all your ways acknowledge Him and He will make your paths straight.

Proverbs 3: 5 (NIV)

When it comes to transformation, God is behind it!

In God's mercy, God can orchestrate man's end. God says that He disciplines those he loves. Through trials, the disciple Paul learned the secret to the peace of God. He stated that he learned to be content in all situations. One interpretation of the Greek word content (or *arkeo*) means acknowledgment of God's control. In an email I received from Dr. Richard Swenson, his closing salutation read, "In His will is His peace." How true!

When it comes to transformation, whether it's the condition of a man's heart, life sustaining order or conducting a series of events so that just the right people show up at just the right time, God is behind it. It is a difficult task to understand God's orchestration of life events and heart transformation. Our finite thinking makes us incapable of really understanding.

If we could somehow capture the mystery, movements and thoughts behind God's actions, we would realize just how far short the detailed transformations in the movie *Transformers* really fall. It really is kids stuff compared to the workings of God. God doesn't orchestrate His transformations with virtual steel, gears and parts. He does it with His power and outstretched arm! Nothing is too difficult for You! Jeremiah 32: 17

If you hear His voice, do not harden your hearts.

Part of our transformation to the likeness of Christ can involve divine tests.[9] Hebrews 4: 7 states, ". . . If you hear His voice, do not harden your hearts." Additionally, Hebrews 3:19 warns, "So we see that they were not able to enter, (rest) because of their unbelief."

Do not be conformed to this world, but be transformed by the renewal of your mind. Then you will be able to test and approve what is the good, pleasing, and perfect will of God.

Romans 12: 2 (BSB)

God demonstrated His awesome power through many miracles, but the Israelites' faith was conditional. The Israelites wanted to live on their terms, not God's. God showed them the parting of the sea, the pillar of fire and He provided meat from heaven and water from rocks! None of these incredible miracles softened their hearts toward God. I believe this is why God isn't so obvious with His miracles today. Heart decisions need to be thought through and, as Paul points out, learned. There needs to be a surrendering of the will and an acknowledgement of His control, no matter what the circumstances or conditions. God is God. No matter how we justify our thinking, we are not gods.

> I believe this is why God isn't so obvious today with His miracles. Heart decisions need to be thought through.

We are not to fear any of God's transitions. A practical way to get destructive fear out of our lives is to gain understanding and knowledge. Transition can be a crisis time for many people. On the contrary, the Chinese definition of crisis is: "a time of opportunity." Under the loving care of our heavenly Father, we are provided exactly that! We are given the opportunity to get to really know our heavenly Father who *is* within our reach.

Life transitions can often come up like a storm, tossing us from here to there. The Bible uses storm imagery several times to reveal certain aspects of God. When the disciples were tossed about in the boat, they were filled with fear for their lives. Talk about a crisis! But God empowered Jesus to calm the storm with his hand and just by uttering a word or two, the sea and the disciples were calm once again. When God spoke to Job in the midst of rain and thunder, Job was enduring a stormy sea of his own. Once the storm retreated, Job's life would be used to glorify his Father. Like Job,

> God is God, no matter how we justify our thinking.

when we are worried or anxious, we can call upon God and we will receive a message of restoration, love and compassion. It is interesting that the book of Psalms, which offers a very soul-soothing message, follows the book of Job with all of his trials.

Job is a great example of how we don't necessarily embrace God's plan for our lives and the lessons He wants to teach us through trials. We live a linear existence and it is difficult for us to see the end of our suffering or to believe that it will result in anything good. We do not like unexpected changes and detours. We prefer a clearly outlined map that takes us around all the troubles! However, it is often the trials that push us to let go of more and more of ourselves, and obtain more and more of Christ. These verses have helped me in keeping a "big picture" perspective.

> Like Job, when we are worried or anxious, we can call upon God and we will receive a message of restoration, love and compassion.

He frustrates the plotting of the shrewd, so that their hands cannot attain success.

Job 5: 12

Blessed indeed is the man whom God corrects; so do not despise the discipline of the Almighty.

Job 5: 17 (BSB)

For You have tried us, O God; You have refined us as silver is refined.

Psalms 66: 10

that the genuineness of your faith, being much more precious than gold that perishes, though it is tested by fire, may be found to praise, honor, and glory at the revelation of Jesus Christ,

I Peter 1: 7 (NKJV)

God knows we are uncomfortable with change. We shouldn't be, but that is the way we are. We should ask why this is the case.

From the time the two cells become one, a heavenly transformation was underway. Today's new scanning technology is able to focus in on the very beginning of human life like never before in detail, clarity and color. Alexander Tsiaras, Associate Professor and Chief of Scientific Visualization of Yale, produced an eye opening conception-to-birth video.[10] Tsiaras' work reveals epic transformation unlike anything anyone has seen before. Tsiaras reveals his reaction to what he found while working on the project:

"The magic of the mechanisms inside each genetic structure saying exactly where that nerve cell should go—the complexity of these, the mathematical models of how these things are indeed done are beyond human comprehension. Even though I'm a mathematician, I look at this with a marvel of how did these instruction sets not make mistakes as they build what is us. It's a mystery, its magic, its divinity."

As an example, Alexander shares what he learned out about collagen, which is found in our skin and hair. "The only place that the collagen *changes* its molecular structure is in the eye. It becomes a grid formation which creates the transparency needed in the covering."

Transformation is in our DNA's original design! It just happens to slow down after age 16 for girls and age 18 for boys, and then stops around 25 (but the change process is still engaged). We are God's biggest and most complex transformer! Is it another design motive to push us to lean on Him?

The mysteries of change are certainly ponderous. We have looked at change in its many forms and we can see how God uses change to transform us and push us towards Him. God-wrought changes can

We are God's biggest and most complex transformer!

> God-wrought changes can put the pressure on each of us to get to know God better and reach new heights in understanding.

put the pressure on each of us to get to know God better and reach new heights in understanding. We are pushed to reach for deeper knowledge and deeper faith. People from all walks of life are called to pursue God, especially in prayer. Whether you are the President of the United States, or a mother up late at night with a colicky baby, you may find yourself getting down on your knees and praying for strength to handle your current difficulties with humility, patience and grace. Through change, we become fully aware of our limitations and realize that we need help from on high. When our backs are against the wall, when we are out of strength and answers, we finally call on our Creator and pray. That's just where God wants us. He wants us to depend on Him through faith and fully trust in Him—every single day!

Our faith journey is filled with transitions. . . We move from a human center of understanding, based on man's point of view, to a new center of understanding based on God's point of view—and God's point of view can give us an eternal perspective!

> We move from a human center of understanding, based on man's point of view, to a new center of understanding based on God's point of view— and God's point of view can give us an eternal perspective!

perspective! It takes some getting used to, but as we pursue knowledge of our Creator, His Word performs its work within us (I Thessalonians 2:13).

That's very exciting! When all things become new, we have access to peace in all situations, perspective in chaos, order in disorder and hope of promises to come.

All Scripture is inspired by God and profitable for teaching, for reproof, for correction, for training in righteousness; so that the man of God may be adequate, equipped for every good work.

II Timothy 3: 16–17

Transforming a Generation

God created the arts and it's beneficial to use these gifts for equipping and inspiring others. The Bible Project (TBP), of Portland Oregon is another example of a modern day transformer. They present the Bible in a relevant manner. The Strategic Partnership Coordinator of TBP has announced that on November 27, 2018 they reached the 1 Million Subscriber mark, and has had over 100 Million views!

The creative team produces animation story lines in a motion-graphic format including copy-text, paintings, graphics and sound effects. The animation presentations are progressively built, in sync with narration. All elements and key messages are designed and art directed with theological oversight.

Their vision: "We want to see a permanent and worldwide change in people's paradigm of the Bible." TBP's team offers the content for free and is crowd-funded. These colorful animation shorts can be viewed online at www.the-bibleproject.com, YouTube and on Amazon's Firestick.

Underlining seems out of place - it begins late in the book, not throughout.

12
Hope in the Passion Creator

In his observations of conception, Alexander Tsiaras brings attention to a molecular communication. Alexander remarks, "when a fertilized egg burrows and connects itself to the side of uterine wall, cell to cell communications commence. 'I am here to stay; plant me.' The estrogen and progesterone cells hear this call and respond!" The cells have been quiet for many years in the women's life until this call. The cells were programmed and designed to respond upon the call from the fertilized egg.[1]

The instruction sets are written in the cells! No wonder we don't want to read the instructions when we are trying to put something together. It's innate with us! The mother's womb is designed to offer this new life everything it needs. Warmth, protection, circulation, nutrients, oxygen and a host of other life-giving elements are in place to do what they were programmed to do at just the right time. The Psalmist writes, "You knit me together in my mother's womb" and Matthew states that "He knows the number of hairs on our heads."

With the help of the Holy Spirit (whom we can have by just asking through prayer), we can wrap our minds around Jesus Christ's presence at the beginning of the universe and our own inception. His loving care for us is intimately written in all of existence. *When Jesus creates, it's all about us. When we see Jesus' hand in creation, it's all about Him!*

> When Jesus creates, it's all about us. When we see Jesus' hand in creation, it's all about Him!

> All that God has planned for us is set in motion when we commit to Him.

Like the fertilized egg securely embedded in the mother's womb, so too can your hope be embedded in what scripture calls the vine. "I am the vine, you are the branches; he who abides in Me and I in him, he bears much fruit, for apart from Me you can do nothing."[2]

Just like our life-giving cells that know exactly what to do at just the right time, all that God has planned for us is set in motion when we commit to Him. John 3:36 reads, "He who believes in Me will have eternal life." The Greek definition of believe is to "commit and adhere to." John writes in John 1: 1, "In the beginning was the Word, and the Word was with God, and the Word was God." Committing and adhering to Jesus, who is the Word of God, is the only safe place to rest your hope.

The Other Side of Heaven

Because of sin, humanity is far from perfect. We're sad when we see people who claim to be Christians acting like hypocrites. When something terrible happens to a friend or family member, we wonder how a loving God can permit bad things to happen to good people. Yes, we will see evil on earth; we are on the wrong side of heaven. Until Jesus comes again, there will always be evil on the earth. It is hard for us to accept, especially when we get a glimpse of our loving Father, and naturally expect His love to permeate all earth and humanity. But humanity is fallen and the earth cursed. The Father has given us a choice: accept Christ and find comfort or dismiss Him and walk alone. Through the sacrifice of Christ, we are not alone. Until Jesus returns, evil will reign on the earth, so we must fix our eyes, our hope and our trust in Him.

> Who would think that our home would be a dangerous battlefield for our soul?

This side of heaven is our current residence. Who would think that our home would be a dangerous battlefield for our soul? If we believe in God, we have to understand that He is a just and transcendent God. When it comes to our souls, God plays hardball. His love for us is not about making us happy, but about making us holy. Earlier we discovered that God wants us to have an intimate, trusting relationship with Him. Satan would like us to believe that God doesn't love us, that God has turned His back on us because God is not giving us what *we* want. Satan wants us to

> Satan wants us to doubt God. Satan wants us to feel abandoned, alone and cold, sulking in the corner and muttering that life isn't fair.

doubt God. Satan wants us to feel abandoned, alone and cold, sulking in the corner and muttering that life isn't fair. Satan used this same strategy in the Garden of Eden and even tried this tactic with Jesus in the desert.

I was there not long ago. Satan was winning and I couldn't see it. I was on a downward slope, heading into a valley of despair and ultimately, facing a spiritual death. In fact, I was so low that it could have led me to my physical death. It wasn't until this moment that I recognized the deep trust and hope I needed to have in

> I could not make one simple creation, like a blade of grass, from absolutely nothing.

my loving God. I remember reminding myself that I could not make one simple creation, like a blade of grass, from absolutely nothing. It reminded me of the design of creation and that my sustained existence is a concern of my Creator. The thoughts of my Creator kept my perspective and kept me alive.

The trial really challenged me in issues of faith. I had years of volunteering for church and parachurch organizations under my belt. I had done award-winning work for many well-known blue-chip companies. I believed that this work entitled me to God's blessings in everything.

> Reading and memorizing verses like these helped to give me the right perspective.

Little did I know that a death by 1,000 cuts was just around the corner. Several key business contacts relocated. I kept loyal employees on the payroll too long. Design software miraculously turned personal computers into design studios and the economy came to a halt. I did not have the business acumen or training to turn this around quickly. Even if I had, I don't know how much it would have helped because so much of it was out of my control. What I also found difficult was the lack of understanding among non-business owners and business owners in other markets. When there is a downturn in the economy, design communication and advertising firms are usually the first industries to feel it. Needless to say, I felt very distant from God and the world! I took it all personally and began to feel like a modern day leper. I remember the local newspaper carrier forgiving our debt to us. At the time, it felt like the most merciful thing anyone had ever done for me. Life did not feel fair.

The behaviors that helped me get through were scripture reading and memory. Verses like: "it rains on the just and unjust," Matthew 5: 45; "He who began a good work in you will perfect it," Philippians 1: 6; "He hears our cries and answers them," Psalm 34: 17, gave me hope. "He gives good gifts to those who ask," Matthew 7: 11; and that "I am more valuable than birds and God takes care of them." Matthew 6: 26; "God is my refuge and my strength, a very present help in times of trouble," Psalm 46: 1, These verses gave me reassurance. Reading and memorizing verses like these helped to give me the right perspective.

> God is the "living water" that quenches the thirst for those that recognize that they are thirsty.

The incredible acts of kindness by loving faithful believers, along with the prayers of many, were much needed reminders of God's care and provision during this time. These reminders helped to hold my faith in a surrendered state. Indeed, God's ways are not our ways. If going through trials is the price we must pay to be able to "see" the passion that God has for us, then the price is fitting! The promised peace that Jesus offers which transcends all understanding, will guard our hearts and minds in Christ Jesus, Philippians 4: 7.

But the tough times can be difficult! The desert's heat is beyond uncomfortable. The thirst is unbearable. This desolate place can carry unimaginable loneliness and despair. Adam and Eve were once in the lush garden of God's love, but they made their own choice and were turned out to work the barren land with sweat and tears. Because of that, we now live by the sweat of the brow until He comes again. The desert, though it can be a place of hardship on this side of heaven, is also a place where God meets His people. God is the "living water" that quenches thirst for those who recognize they are thirsty.

His plan includes life coming at us with full force. Yielding to the Creator is the first step. Next, we need to accept that life events can bring us closer to God. It's up to us to engage with Him. This is what makes the journey a challenge and redemption exciting. It's all worth it if we look to our *real* home—in heaven!

> His plan includes life coming at us with full force.

A Passionately and Creatively Prepared Place

Prior to Jesus' ascension into heaven, He told us that he would go and "prepare a place" for us, John 14: 3. The operative word here is "prepare." The Preparer is the one who ushered in the universe. Heaven is described in specific terms: "No eye has seen, no ear has heard, no mind has conceived what God has prepared for those who love him."[3] OK, this is inconceivable. In the book of Revelation, the Apostle John speaks of the Revelation of the Lord Jesus Christ. He tells us of the New Jerusalem, a city with roads made of gold, walls made of rubies and gates made of pearls. Not having Satan around will be joy enough for me. But wait, there's more! God promises that in His mansion there are many rooms. Scripture also gives physical dimensions of the new kingdom to come.

I believe we get a better idea of heaven when we look at our Creator with His "beyond understanding" attributes. We know He operates outside this dimension and is separated from our concepts of time,

> Jesus is not bound in any way by what we see, hear, touch or sense.

space, mass, and energy. He used a handful of elements to create life. Scripture states, "He is before all things and in Him all things hold together," Colossians 1: 17. Jesus is not bound in any way by what we see, hear, touch or sense. He is Master of the microbial and God of the galaxies.

There are so many questions I have about our real home. Will God have a new color we haven't ever seen? Will He use a new raw element base? Will there be new musical instruments or will our hearing be newly tuned so that we will be able to hear sounds that have always been around us? Will we have any of His divine abilities, such as walking on water or turning water into wine?

> Will God have a new color we haven't ever seen? Will He use a new raw element base? Will we be able to hear sounds that have always been around us?

God told us there was going to be a banquet upon arrival. Well I am glad to hear that there will be food! What is a church gathering without food? I can't imagine the flavors. Talk about flavor enhancers! Will there be new types of veggies or fruit? And how about steaks? The most exciting thing my finite mind (and stomach) can hope for would be brand new flavors of ice cream! If you think Ben and Jerry's have some neat flavors, hang on to your halos!

I get such a kick out of smells, like the smell of fresh ground coffee beans in a coffee shop! Will

> He is the Master of the microbial and God of the galaxies.

there be a new heavenly bean to grind? My wife is a big fan of teas. Put on your creative cap and try to name a few of the terrific tasting teas that wait for us at the banquet of a lifetime!

There have to be flowers in heaven. And I hope our smell receptors can hold onto a scent longer than five seconds! The scent of blooming carnations, roses, lilacs, and perhaps brand new hybrids, all in bloom in the mansion's beautiful green house. . . all year long. I can't imagine it! Our Master Creator is beyond what is imaginable!

A Passionate Prayer, A Passionate Praise

My son is a member of the 'digital native' group that was discussed earlier. My wife and I have been very comfortable with praying often. For us, it is a way of life. Our son is at an age where we feel he needs to start to go a little deeper in his faith walk. The challenge is before us. What can he relate to that shows the power of prayer?

Another hurdle to overcome is my son's current belief that God doesn't answer prayer. He has witnessed what we went through, our struggles and frustrations. The heartbreak I still feel today. I hope his faith will be intact in a future writing. It is written,

> *I will destroy the wisdom of the wise; the*
> *intelligence of the intelligent I will frustrate.*

I Corinthians 1: 19 (BSB)

After a few years of divine hammering, I was just beginning to learn about the obey part, and that God expects me to actually practice what I am learning! Unfortunately, we could only shelter our son so much from the harsh realities of life. When my teenaged son asked for things, such as a fishing trip, a dirt bike and new expensive clothing but didn't get them, he blamed God. Finally, when the family had to sell the four-wheeler, it was the end of all things from his teenage perspective.

We all have preconceived ideas about deity. These ideas stem from our childhood. Some of us spend a lifetime gathering and summarizing our experiences to reach our

God expects me to actually practice what I am learning!

> We all have preconceived ideas about deity. These ideas stem from our childhood.

current belief system. Others may come to the table after experiencing destructive situations or may come from dysfunctional families. Sin can steer our ship into these rocky shores, but often, we just aren't vigilant enough to avoid the dangerous shipwrecks. Unaddressed hurts, inflicted by others, can become the bitterness that eats away at our hearts like the saltwater waves that hammer the deck of a ship. Whether a victim or an offender, justifying and solidifying our stance can be like an anchor that weighs us down. We are no longer free. We are unable to sail. Satan is pleased that we cannot see the lighthouse of Christ that guides us home. We are prevented from being as God intended us to be: His pure, undefiled, God-breathed Creations. God wants us to set a course for a place where we are clean and free from sin—humbly bowed before our Captain and life-Designer.

> What's alarming about this is that when we were young children with untrained minds, we were inadvertently wiring ourselves into our belief systems of today.

Some of us are physically hardwired to our negative experiences. Scientists now have the ability to observe the hardwiring that happens on a molecular level in our brains.[4] This negative thinking isn't just a result of a negative outlook, but can stem from traumatic life experiences, physical or emotional abuse from peers, friends, family and caregivers, and can result in repetitive toxic self-talk. Through video presentations, Dr. Caroline Leaf demonstrates exactly how the rewiring of our brain cells physically form new connections on self-perception. Our brain cells shift, build and connect to accommodate repetitive thinking patterns. We literally hardwire ourselves to our understandings of situations, experiences, good, bad and even the nonsensical.

What's alarming about this is that when we were young children with untrained minds, we were inadvertently wiring ourselves into our belief systems of today.

> *Train up a child in the way he should go,*
> *Even when he is old he will not depart from it.*

Proverbs 22: 6

As adults, how many have had training in high school (or even in college) on how to handle social media slander, sexual violations, abuse, neglect or addictions in any form? Our changing society is leaving children and adults exposed and unprepared for events and situations such as these. Deep heart-hurts are left unattended. God desires to address and <u>heal</u> these. One example of this hardwired concept is explained by the admonition of the Hebrews in the Bible:

> *Look after each other so that none of you fails to receive*
> *the grace of God. Watch out that no poisonous root of bit-*
> *terness grows up to trouble you, corrupting many.*

Hebrews 12: 15 (NLT)

> *See to it that no one comes short of the grace*
> *of God; that no root of bitterness spring-*
> *ing up causes trouble, and by it be defiled;*

Hebrews 12: 15

I have used two different translations of the same verse to give a better understanding of what the author is telling us. Psychologists say that ninety percent of counseling cases involve unresolved issues due to unforgiveness. The word "root" is an appropriate metaphor for what bitterness does to our souls. A root relates to the subterranean—below the surface; what is not visible but spreads relentlessly. As I have mentioned before, in our farming days we've had our share of weeds. I have spoken of the Canada Thistle, but let me tell you about bamboo. It spreads through its root system. You pull one up and can follow the connecting root to the next plant and the next and so on. That is how bitterness spreads in our hearts. If we don't stop it in its tracks it will spring up and cause us all kind of trouble in many different areas of our lives. For starters bitterness can destroy relationships as well as negatively affect our physiology all the way down to our DNA. Dr. Leaf claims that severe illnesses can be caused from this. God gave us a very appropriate analogy in the use of the word root—toxic thoughts grow.

> Should our fallen perspectives dictate our eternity and have power to influence our relationship with God?

Our Adamic nature (given to us upon Adam and Eve's rebellion) is bent toward sin, resentment, and bitterness. We seek out the negative and untrue. We are fascinated with reality shows that really do a good job of demonstrating our fallen nature. We give a sigh of relief and swipe our hand across our brow when the cop and the flashing lights pass us and pull over another car. We say to ourselves "Whew, glad that's not me!" This is a natural response for our fleshly nature. But our flesh is not to rule us! We are to respond in a way contrary to our nature. We are to respond like Christ. What would that look like? "I am thankful that the speeder did not hurt someone or get in an accident. Maybe the officer will exhibit mercy, and maybe the speeder will have learned a lesson." As comical as this response may sound, it demonstrates our Adamic nature and its life-altering roots!

The question arises: Do these fallen perspectives dictate our eternity and have power to influence our relationship with God? Yes they do. The roots of negative experiences can keep us from seeing reality and truth.

It also can take away hope. This alone is life threatening. When we lose our hope, our will to live is threatened. Our life purpose is gone. Unfortunately, this is where suicide becomes an option. And, fortunately, a new choice presents itself...

When we lose our hope, our will to live is threatened.

..Hope in the Passionate Creator. Not hope in our present circumstance, what we've lost, or our abilities, but hope in Creator God. If we can recognize that our physical wiring—thinking and reasoning, is unable to see, feel or sense hope, then this is the most life-threatening place to be. This is also the worst time ever to make a big decision.

If we can muster up enough strength to have a mustard seed-size of faith and hope, we can begin to see the power of God begin to work.

And the God of all grace, who called you to his eternal glory in Christ, after you have suffered a little while, will himself restore you and make you strong, firm and steadfast.

I Peter 5: 10 (NIV)

For in this hope we were saved; but hope that is seen is no hope at all. Who hopes for what he can already see? But if we hope for what we do not yet see, we wait for it patiently.

Romans 8: 24–25 (BSB)

Yet those who wait for the LORD Will gain new strength; They will mount up with wings like eagles, They will run and not get tired, They will walk and not become weary.

Isaiah 40: 31

Sound Christian counseling and God's Word can restore a forgiving nature and help us begin to see all that God has to offer us—including restoring hope. Since we are three parts, mind, <u>body</u> and spirit, medications maybe be helpful to assist with the rewiring. Exercising can help to burn of excess stress chemicals which can hinder healing.

These life situations can be too large for one person to handle. Try not to manage them alone. There are others that have gone down similar paths and can share their experiences with you.

Forgave And Gave Up

Jesus' passionate prayer when being put to death was "Forgive them Father, for they know not what they do," Luke 23: 34. This prayer has protection in its intent and the act has passion in its purpose. Jesus knew of the persecutor's Adamic sin nature. He knew of the personal baggage and the condition of the hearts of all involved in His death.

Jesus knew that they were lost and hurt children making wrong decisions .

Jesus gave up His right for justice and instead made us the priority by becoming the final sacrifice for our sins. Jesus saw His persecutors' frailty. He saw past their condemned condition, their rags of guilty works. Maybe they were not *redemption worthy,* but Christ saw them as *worth redeeming!* Christ entreated

> God knows of our hardwiring! He knows exactly how each brain receptor is connected, rerouted and/or disconnected.

the heavenly Father's compassion and understanding and asked Him to forgive his killers for their horrific deed, as Christ had not yet died to pay the penalty for it. Is it possible for us to acknowledge that we are just as frail as our predecessors, that we are just as depraved in our hearts? To acknowledge this is to realize our need for a savior.

God tells us that above all else, we need to guard our hearts, proverbs 4: 23. Our hearts were initially designed to love God. To pray passionately, we need to get real with ourselves and care about God's initial design of our hearts. His desire for us was to have hearts that are sensitive to the things of God and to Christ's soul cleansing work on the cross.

> But He was wounded for our transgressions, He was-
> bruised for our iniquities; The chastisement for our peace
> was upon Him, And by His stripes we are healed.
>
> Isaiah 53: 4–5 (NKJV)

> We now have an eternal home in Heaven and we are privileged heirs and children of the King!

The penalty for turning our hearts away from God and choosing sin over Him is death. However, the Bible clearly demonstrates that from death, new life can spring forth. There is a complete reversal of the horrible finality of death and it becomes a glorious renewal!

In the Jewish tradition of the Passover, the blood of a sacrificed lamb was painted on the doorways to protect them from the angel of death as he visited the land of the Pharaoh. Moses' people were saved. In addition, the frequent practice of sacrificing a lamb at the temple was done to cover the sins of the people. The shedding of an unblemished, innocent lamb satisfied the penalty for sin—temporarily, but had to be repeated over and over. The shedding of the pure, holy, unblemished, innocent blood of *The* Lamb of God satisfied the penalty of all sin: past present and future. Jesus was sent as mankind's perfect sacrifice. Jesus satisfies the debt described in John 3:16. By accepting this free gift, we experience healing in our relationship with the Father and we are restored once again.

We pray to know God. I John reads, "To know God is to fear Him and obey His commands." The Hebrew and Chaldean definition of fear (yare) is to have an awesome respect or reverence for something or someone.[4] Although obedience can be a tough endeavor, God knows of our hardwiring. He knows exactly how each brain receptor is connected. Paul writes that we should work out our salvation with fear and trembling, Philippians 2: 12. Our bad habits and attitudes are not always changed in an instantly. Sometimes God wants us to work things out with Him at our side. Character is built as we renew our old way of thinking. What can be changed in an instant is our eternal destination. Should we choose, we can have an eternal home in heaven and we are privileged heirs of the King!

Considering prayer, why is it necessary to talk about forgiveness? Sin is the divider between man and God. The prayer connection is severed until the sin issue is acknowledged. Understanding that sin separates us from God is the first step to reconnecting with Him.

> *But your iniquities have separated you from your*
> *God; And your sins have hidden His face from you,*
> *So that He will not hear.*

Isaiah 59: 2 (NKJV)

We want our prayers to be unencumbered by man's fallen state. God wants us to know that He didn't create us to live in sin.

> *For all have sinned and fall short of the glory of God...*

Romans 3: 23

God originally created us to be free from sin—no evil desires, greed, disease, covetousness, etc. Adam and Eve, in our stead, made the choice that we all would have made eventually. They chose to disobey God and the penalty for their disobedience was to know good and evil. We know evil and know it all too well. This choice separated Adam and Eve and all of mankind from God. They no longer walked in the garden with their Father. The relationship was broken.

Even in the midst of this broken relationship, God still gave man a way to connect with Him—through prayer. This thread of friendship is found throughout the Bible. Through prayer we have a way to communicate to the Creator of the Universe, the One who put the sun and moon and stars in their place. Why not follow the communication instructions that He left for us?

> *The time is fulfilled, and the kingdom of God is*
> *at hand; repent and believe in the gospel.*
>
> Mark 1: 15

God made you. God made me. The Bible teaches that He knows what we are going to ask before we ask. He is omniscience in its full capacity. God desires to communicate with us—the ones that He was thinking of before the beginning. God wrote your name in the Book of Life! The actual name of this book is: *the book of the life of the Lamb who has been slain*, Revelation 13: 8.

God wants to hear from you. The verses below can help you as you pray. See them as God's personal messages to you. Meditate on them. They are his love letter, written just for you.

> *For God so loved the world, that He gave His*
> *only begotten Son, that whoever believes in Him*
> *shall not perish, but have eternal life.*
>
> John 3: 16

> *Let your gentleness be evident to all. The Lord is near. Do*
> *not be anxious about anything, but in everything, by prayer*
> *and petition, with thanksgiving, present your requests to*
> *God. And the peace of God, which transcends all understand-*
> *ing, will guard your hearts and minds in Christ Jesus.*
>
> Philippians 4: 5–7 (NIV)

You can be upset, hiding something or ashamed. . . it doesn't matter, He knows all about it. Prayer crosses into the spiritual dimension of life. God casts a shadow over your right hand. He is nearby and listening!

If you have prayed the previous verses back to God and the prayers are from your heart, you have prayed a prayer of salvation. You have been saved. Welcome home sister! Welcome home brother!

Just as I was finishing the final chapter of this book, I had a very unusual dream. There was a slightly grayed haired gentleman who seemed to be caught up in his sin. He was handling and shuffling all sorts of very sharp objects. They were in a variety of shapes and sizes; some were shard-like, made of steel or glass, and many of them had handles on them. He started to throw some of these—impaling them into the walls and woodwork. In my dream, I felt threatened and so did the other eight to ten people in the room. The tension rose greatly.

The gentleman seemed to be a father figure at first—someone you could trust. I sensed an intense frustration as he threw the sharp objects. The incident could have easily caused death or injury, but for some reason it didn't cause either.

I was able to detect remorse residing deep in his eyes. Cautiously I asked the man, "Do you feel sorry?" I later interpreted this part of the dream as a deep struggle within, a conflict of the soul that has been buried for a long time, but has now been stirred. There is no apparent way out. The frustration manifested itself with the burst of rage. The gentleman looked at me intently, and his eyes told me that he was remorseful. I then simply said, "Jesus loves you." At that moment the man seemed to surrender his will and became peace filled. The anxiety left the room. Suddenly I awoke, and wondered what were the implications of this dream. I had the impression that these images would have significant meaning for someone else. To be honest, I believe the significance and interpretation of it lies in you, the reader. This is why I am including it in this book. How does this dream speak to you? My wife Tammy gives her interpretation:

"We all have the broken pieces of our lives. They lie on the floor like dangerous shards of glass that we must carefully step around. We wish we could get a handle on them. How much we would like to just be able to grab them and toss them aside. But they don't usually come with handles. However God can use these broken shards as tools for us to grow and learn by. He can put the handles on them so that we can pick them up and examine them and toss them aside for Christ. Often God uses them to draw us to Himself, to get us to finally 'give up' and surrender it all to Him."

Never will I leave you; never will I forsake you.

Hebrews 13: 5 (BSB)

Philippians 4: 9 instructs us to put what we've learned, received or heard into practice. You can start by finding a Bible believing church to attend. Communicate to a church leader where you are in spiritual growth. Share any stumbling blocks that you feel could be hindering your perspective. He or she should be able to point you in an appropriate direction. You may be surprised at how setbacks can be turned into strengths with God's real-world help.

The praise is simple but still just as real and heartfelt as *your passionate prayer.* Thank God for your free gift of salvation, the Kingdom to come and His promise of everlasting life. God is rejoicing over you!

The Lord your God is among you: He is mighty to save.
He will rejoice over you with gladness; He will quiet you
with His love; He will rejoice over you with singing.

Zephaniah 3: 17 (BSB)

There will be a day when God chooses to reveal His Creative ways. . . perhaps it will include the secret of making something out of nothing! I can't wait!

According to Luke 10: 27, Jesus told us that the greatest commandment is: "You shall love the Lord your God with all your heart, and with all your soul, and with all your strength, and with all your mind; and your neighbor as yourself." Life's distractions can quickly capture your heart and find their way into the very core of your being. My prayer is that *Before the Beginning...God Designed* will nurture a desire to really get to *know* your Maker and Designer. He is there for you and me. . . personally! God quietly waits for us to choose to be His friend. He desires that His Spirit, with fire, will flow through us so we can be used in ways we can *never* imagine on our own.

The Renewing of Hearts and Minds

And the peace of God, which transcends all comprehension,
will guard your hearts and your minds in Christ Jesus.

Philippians 4:7

As I end this book I want to spend a few minutes on loving God with all of our hearts and all of our minds. Of great importance to the Lord is for us to guard our hearts. Your heart condition is valued by God, and it should be valued by you!

I heard a voice which said, 'There is one, even
Christ Jesus, that can speak to thy condition', and
when I heard it, my heart did leap for joy.

George Fox, Founder of Friends Church

Through His Word, God is renewing my mind daily. I am asking God to teach me, to show me more of what I need to know. I can only share with you what I know at this time and place on life's journey. God isn't finished with me yet and my journey has not ended. He will continue to mold me into His image and transform my mind and my heart into the likeness of Christ. This book is a snapshot, if you will, of how I see my Maker and eternity at this point in my life. My hope is that it will help you along in yours.

> In my travels I have found that those who keep heaven in view remain serene and cheerful in the darkest day. If the glories of heaven were more real to us, if we lived less for material things and more for things eternal and spiritual, we would be less easily disturbed by this present life.

> Billy Graham, American Evangelist

In chapter 12, I talked about my son's need to go deeper with his faith and His need to see God work in his daily life. Well, that is being addressed ever so miraculously, as I finish this book. My son sees us pray and the Lord provide while we do this work. The Lord is redeeming us by answering prayer, guarding my son's heart, my daughter's heart, and my wife's heart. In God's own special ways, He has personally ministered to my heart.

Now that I am in the process of answering His call, I can proclaim in confidence that God is my redeemer! And even as I write this closing, it's not an easy time, but my family is still seeing miracle after miracle. We are now looking forward to seeing God work by getting this book into the right hands.

By God's mercy, if you can recognize, acknowledge and *accept* God's desire to love each one of us through His Son Jesus Christ *and His* creation, you will see God's epic passion displayed on a personal level.

When you see God's creative touch on your life, your loved ones' lives, and all that He put into place to perfectly care for us all, your

> When you see God's creative touch on your life, your loved ones' lives, and all that He put into place to perfectly care for us, your perspective changes.

perspective changes. With a new perspective we can more easily accept the ups and downs of life. It reminds us that God is in control and He will walk beside us through the barren places as well as the fertile ones. We can accept other's differences because God made them, loves them and forgives them. Knowing we are not yet perfected in Christ, we can accept others just as God accepts us the way we are.

In 1965, Paul Harvey, a conservative American radio broadcaster, gave an address called, "If I Were the Devil." Mr. Harvey stated that the devil is actively seizing our hearts, our very being. Search in YouTube: "If I Were the Devil", and see if you have fallen into the 'do as you please' attitude toward life. You will see that most of Mr. Harvey's contrast-creating words still ring true today. Our nation has been drifting away from the things of God for a long time. However, many are turning to God and seeing our Creator care for their hearts as well.

> When you know what God has done for you, the power
> and the tyranny of sin is gone and the radiant, unspeakable
> emancipation of the indwelling Christ has come.
>
> Oswald Chambers

> Is the glory of God the most precious
> treasure on the horizon of your future?
>
> John Piper

He reveals Himself generally through His creation, especially through His Word, and ultimately through His Son[1] If we consider what it took in creativity, sensitivity, forethought and transcendent genius in design and planning to create the world around us, we find hope and a more *eternal perspective*. Understanding the love God demonstrated to us in His provisional design of creation and His personal interest in our hearts can give us encouragement and comfort. We *can* experience awe and wonder on this side of heaven, reflecting on everything as it was intended to be, *before* the beginning and again when His Kingdom comes.

Addendum

I would like to spend a few pages addressing the peer review process and narratives. If a scientific claim had to go through a US court of law, it would likely fail. According to the American Physiological Society, there are many weaknesses in the system that make it possible to generate misleading information in the area of professional peer reviews, see the list below. The current process lacks accountability.

Information made in the sciences that is misleading or fraudulent, is detrimental to society. Generally the public trusts science, however, as research equipment advances in its capabilities, it is revealing an alternate narrative. Concealing discovered facts to continue a dated paradigm, such as evolution, puts students and researchers on an imaginary story line. The public leaves reality and enters into an era of irresponsibility.

- No formal training is required for the reviewer. The reviewer learns on the job.
- Bias is present in peer and includes job pressures. If you give a bad review, it is likely that you, the reviewer, won't be asked again. This can lead to loss of objectivity.
- Reviewing is like any other skill; you get better with practice.
- It's hard to find experts on certain subjects, therefore it is easy to make mistakes.
- School textbook writers and researchers pick up these articles and publishers print them, without scrutiny.
- Intentionally delayed "stonewalled" reviews exist because the reviewer is trying to get published first on the subject.
- Scientific merit is compromised when political interest, business or potential sales outcomes of books and maga-

zines influence the reviewer's opinion.

- Uncovering corruption/scientific misconduct is difficult at best.
- Biases exist toward certain authors.
- Trust has been damaged and weakened in the scientific community's review process.[1]

Since the *scientific community* sees that its monitoring process is faulty, it stands to reason that some outcomes and scientific claims cannot (and should not) be fully trusted in academia or industry. At the very least, added scrutiny should be applied.

Just as there should be more careful analysis of information that we take in, we need to simultaneously scrutinize information we distribute. The quality of validation depends on many variables, such as a subject's importance or relevance, who may be positively or negatively affected by this information and in what way.

Our output needs to show integrity. If we are presenting information, we are to make every effort to ensure accuracy. We need to work towards achieving factual truth and objectivity.

At a recent lunch, I happened to overhear a gentleman sitting next to me was an instructor and an author. When he got up to leave, I asked him what he taught. He said he was a professor at one of the local universities and he taught anatomy and physiology. I told him I was writing a book and one of the chapters I was working on happened to be about peer-reviewed information. He knew exactly where I was going and jumped in with his recent textbook error-catching experiences. He went on to say the textbooks recently acquired are filled with errors. It was very frustrating for him to be teaching one thing while the textbook was stating something else. This frustration undoubtedly faces many educators at all levels of education throughout our nation!

On our current path, in order for evolutionary theories to be removed or changed in our school textbooks, evolutionary proponents literally have to die off.[2] The peer review process should also reflect what our courts use to verify information. Perhaps a few rules from the

Federal Rules of Evidence could be included. Here are four that would be helpful:

Rule # 614	. . . All parties are entitled to cross-examine witnesses thus called.
Rule # 702	. . . May testify thereto in the form of an opinion or otherwise, if (1) the testimony is based upon sufficient facts or data, (2) the testimony is the product of reliable principles and methods, and (3) the witness has applied the principles and methods reliably to the facts of the case.
Rule #703	. . . Facts or data that are otherwise inadmissible shall not be disclosed to the jury by the proponent of the opinion or inference unless the court determines that their probative value in assisting the jury to evaluate the expert's opinion substantially outweighs their prejudicial effect.
Rule #705	. . . The expert may in any event be required to disclose the underlying facts or data on cross examination.[3]

The peer review process is under increased pressure as scientific journals burgeon due to added research funding. In many instances, editors are no longer experts and US federal agency has loosened peer review rules.[4] This dynamic will only lead to additional unfounded or dated science printed in our textbooks and posted on line.

A Paradigm Shift for the Better.

When *peer-reviewed article* is printed or posted by a credible source, it is cited as well. As tidy as this looks, there are significant holes in this system that can cause a number of problems—all of which can take the reader down the wrong track. So in short, if the information presented is misleading or distorted, it can go undetected. If the reader gets off track, good observable evidence can be ignored. If we are basing our work on a shaky foundation, it can easily crumble later on. Truth is always the best route.

We don't want to wait for the contributors to die off before we change the textbooks. This is the current path our society is on. And most importantly, it is a disservice to our children, hindering good discovery and impeding them from learning all that God has for them to discover about His world. *Let their parents teach it.*

Separation of church + state

...an idea for colleges is to design and write a degree or certification program on the administration of the peer review process.

To help funnel and guide the present information overload, an idea for colleges is to design and create a certification program on the administration of the peer review process. We want good, solid information filtering down to our textbooks so our kids don't have to wade through a sea of unverifiable and misleading information. A program like this could help and would create some jobs as well.

Charles Darwin's *On the Origin of Species*, written in 1859, has become the foundation of evolutionary biology. A recent work by Nathaniel T. Jeanson, BS, PhD, *Replacing Darwin*, written in 2017, is a technical read on microbiology. The thought provoking book presents challenges to the model of random chance origins; academia would do well to include *Replacing Darwin* and other like books in their curriculums.

Finally, brethren, whatever is true, whatever is honorable, whatever is right, whatever is pure, whatever is lovely, whatever is of good repute, if there any excellence and if anything worthy of praise, dwell on these things.

Philippians 4: 8

Preface

1. Nicholas Giordano, Suffolk Community College Professor. *Reason for Violence*, accessed November 29, 2018, https://www.youtube.com/watch?v=MM_RYB3y-i0. Viewing start time: 26:45
2. Fromm, Erich. (1956). *The Art of Loving*, (New York: Harper & Row).
3. Arron Armstrong, August 15, 2018 Article, accessed December 5, 2018, https://www.gospelproject.com/god-shows-tells/
4. Tim Mackie, Ph.D., The Bible Project

Introduction

1. Dr. Caroline *Leaf*, Ph.D., Communication Pathology, BSc in Logopedics and Audiology, *Through Her Eyes - The Sower And The Seed*, accessed December 5, 2018, https://www.youtube.com/watch?v=YiXP_gBMPYs
2. RC Sproul, founder of Ligonier Ministries, Pastor, *The Holiness of God*, (Carlol Stream, IL, Tyndale House).
3. John Piper, American Reformed Baptist continuationist pastor and author, founder of desiringGod.org *Why Did God Create the World?*, sermon accessed August 5, 2019, https://www.desiringgod.org/messages/why-did-god-create-the-world

I: What Was He Thinking?

1. I Corinthians 2: 8–16, New American Standard (NAS).
2. John 15: 15, (NAS).
3. Dr. Werner Gitt, *In the beginning was information*, [sic], (Master Books, Green Forest, AZ, 2007).
4. Richard A. Swenson, M.D., *More Than Meets The Eye*, (Nav Press, Colorado Springs, CO, 2000), 73.
5. I Peter 1: 6, 7, (NAS).
6. Philip Yancey and Dr. Paul Brand, *In the Likeness of God*, (Zondervan, Grand Rapids, MI, 2004), 349.

7.   Philip Yancey and Dr. Paul Brand, *In the Likeness of God*, 353.

8.   Richard A. Swenson, M.D., *More Than Meets The Eye*, 38.

9.   Richard A. Swenson, M.D., *More Than Meets The Eye*, 39.

10.   Richard A. Swenson, M.D., *More Than Meets The Eye*, 40.

11.   The Free Dictionary, *Passion*, accessed November 28, 2018, http://www.the-freedictionary.com/passion.

12.   Mark Batterson, *Primal*, (Multnomah Books, New York, NY, 2010), 7.

13.   Sam A. Smith, "Who Wrote 'the Psalms of David?", 2012, *The Biblical Reader*, accessed November 28, 2018, http://www.biblicalreader.com/btr/Who_Wrote_the_Psalms_of_David.htm.

14.   Isaiah 42: 21, I Corinthians 1: 21.

15.   Dr. Jobe Martin, *Incredible Creatures that Defy Evolution I*, DVD.

16.   ABC News, *Terri Irwin's 20/20 Interview with Barbara Walters*," September 27, 2006.

17.   II Chronicles 7: 14 (NAS)

2: God's Heart In Communication With Man's Heart

1.   Hans Walter Wolff, *Anthropology of the Old Testament* (Fortress Press, Philadelphia, PA, 1975), 40.

2.   Luke 8: 14, (NAS).

3: Inspirations of God

1.   Elizabeth Dougherty, MIT School of Engineering, *What are thoughts made of?*, accessed August 1, 2018, (https://engineering.mit.edu/engage/ask-an-engineer/what-are-thoughts-made-of/).

2.   Dr. Jason Lisle, *Taking back Astronomy, The Heavens Declare Creation and Science Confirms It*, (Master Books, Green Forest, AZ, 2006), 33, AiG Bookstore: https://answersingenesis.org/store/product/taking-back-astronomy/.

3.   Encyclopedia Britanica, *Strong Force*. A fundamental interaction of nature that acts between subatomic particles of matter. The strong force binds quarks together in clusters to make more-familiar subatomic particles, such as protons and neutrons. It also holds together the atomic nucleus and underlies interactions between all particles containing quarks. Accessed November 28, 2018, http://www.britannica.com/EBchecked/topic/569442/strong-force.

4.   Encyclopedia Britanica, *Golden Ratio*, also known as the golden section, golden mean, or divine proportion, in mathematics, the irrational number $(1 + \sqrt{5})/2$, often denoted by the Greek letters τ or ϕ, and approximately

equal to 1.618.) Accessed November 28, 2018, http://www.britannica.com/search?query=golden+ratio.

5. Genesis 6: 5–6, Hosea 11: 7–8, Ephesians 4: 30–31, (NAS).

4: God's Creation: Get the Message

1. Sweet Light: A photographer's term used to describe a quality of light that can only occur at sunrise as well as late in the day around sunset. The sun's angle is such that the rays travel through a higher concentration of atmospheric particles, adding either the soft pastel look or a glowing quality.
2. Richard A. Swenson, M.D., *More Than Meets The Eye*, 37.
3. CBS News, *Deep Sea Volcanic Vent May Offer Discoveries*, accessed November 28, 2018, http://www.cbsnews.com/2100-205_162-6388402.html.
4. Alaska Public Lands Information Centers, *Ice Worms*, accessed November 28, 2018, http://www.alaskacenters.gov/ice-worms.cfm.
5. Dr. Jason Lisle, *Taking back Astronomy, The Heavens Declare Creation*, 17.
6. Dr, Jason Lisle, *Taking back Astronomy, The Heavens Declare Creation*, 16.
7. Baskin Robbins is a registered trademark of BR IP Holder LLC.
8. Paul Garner, *The New Creationism*, (EP Books, Carlisle, PA, 2009), 134.
9. Dr. Jobe Martin, *Incredible Creatures that Defy Evolution III*, DVD.
10. Dr. Werner Gitt, *In the beginning was information,* [sic] 18

5: Diversity and Devotion

1. Ecclesiastes 12: 13, (NAS).
2. Psalm 139: 15, (NAS).

6: The Garden Around Us

1. Richard Swenson, MD., *More Than Meets The Eye*, 38.
2. Acts 17; 24–28, Job 12: 10, Hebrews 1: 3, (NAS).
3. Ephesians 1: 4, (NAS).
4. I Timothy 6: 17, (NAS).

7: 1.2 oz.–2,000 lb. Beasts

1. McDonald's is a registered trademark of McDonald's Corporation.
2. TCBY is a registered trademark of Mrs. Fields Famous Brands: Dairy Queen is a registered trademark of AM.D.Q. CORP. Ben and Jerry's is a registered trademark of *Ben & Jerry's* Homemade, Inc.

3. Outback is a registered trademark of Bloomin' Brands, Inc. LoneStar is a registered trademark of Lone Star Texas Grill.

4. Jim Carrey interview, *Inside the Actors Studio*, hosted by James Lipton, season 17, episode 2, original airdate: 2011-01-10.

5. Vance Ferrell, *Marvel of God's Creation #1* (Harvestime Books, Altamont, TN, no publishing date offered).

6. CBSNEWS, *Deep Sea Volcanic Vent May Offer Discoveries*, April 12, 2010, accessed November 28, 2018, http://www.cbsnews.com/2100-205_162-6388402.html.

7. Ferrell, *Marvel of God's Creation #6*. Accessed November 28, 2018, http://biblicaldiscipleship.org/content/marvel-god%E2%80%99s-creation-6-angler-fish

8. Ferrell, *Marvel of God's Creation #10*. Accessed November 28, 2018, http://biblicaldiscipleship.org/content/marvel-god%E2%80%99s-creation-10-woodpecker

9. National Malleefowl Recovery Team, accessed November 28, 2018, http://www.nationalmalleefowl.com.au/malleefowl-facts.html.

8: The Masters and Masterpieces

1. J.K. Rowling stated that one day she would be "found out" in a recorded interview at the Roald *Dahl* Museum in Buckinghamshire, United Kingdom, personal visit July, 2005.

2. Michael J. Gelb, *How To Think Like Leonardo da Vinci*, (Dell Publishing Group, New York, NY, 2000), acccessed November 28, 2018, http://www.michaelgelb.com.

3. Michael J. Gelb, *How To Think Like Leonardo da Vinci*, 47.

4. Philippians 3: 13, (NAS).

5. John 15: 5, Galatians 5: 1, (NAS).

6. II Corinthians 5: 17, (NAS).

7. John 8: 32, Psalm 51: 12, (NAS).

8. II Corinthians 3: 18, (NAS).

9. Richard Deem, Evidence For God, *Did Albert Einstein Believe in a Personal God?*, accessed November 28, 2018, http://www.godandscience.org/apologetics/einstein.html.

10. Daniel S. Burt, *The biography book: a reader's guide to nonfiction, fictional, and film biographies of more than 500 of the most fascinating individuals of all time.* (Greenwood Publishing Group, 2001), 315.

11. James R. Graham, *The Early Period* (1608–1672), 250.

12. Webb, R.K., Knud Haakonssen, *The Emergence of Rational Dissent*;

Enlightenment and Religion: Rational Dissent in eighteenth-century Britain, (Cambridge University Press, Cambridge, England, 1996), 19.

13. Dr. Werner Gitt, *In the beginning was information,* [sic], 105.

14. Austin Brown, The Long Foundation, *Long Term Art, The Lost (and Found?) Battle of Anghiari,* states, ". . . a story that could likely be behind the hiding of the Fresco. The painting was experimental as DaVinci was working on a new paint pigment. Published May 16, 2012, accessed November 28, 2018, http://blog.longnow.org/02012/05/16/the-lost-and-found-battle-of-anghiari/.

15. Philip Yancey and Dr. Paul Brand, *In the Likeness of God,* 533.

16. Austin Brown, The Long Foundation, "Long Term Art", *The Lost (and Found?) Battle of Anghiari,* Notation found in paragraph 9.

9: Unveiling Creation Design

1. National Geographic, *Brain Games,* accessed November 28, 2018, http://natgeotv.com/ca/brain-games/videos/switcheroo.

2. Deuteronomy 11: 19, Ephesians 6: 4, Deuteronomy 4: 9.

10: Obstacles That Keep Us From God's Passion

1. Jeffrey Tomkins, Ph.D., Institute for Creation Research, *Gene Control Regions Are Protected—Negating Evolution,* accessed November 28, 2018, www.icr.org/article/6886/.

2. YouTube, "Antony Flew's conversion to theism," accessed November 28, 2018 https://www.youtube.com/watch?v=52CyiM0uiWE.

3. Garner, *The New Creationism,* 13.

4. Dr. Heribert Nilson, professor at Lund University, *Synthetische Artbildung* The Synthetic Formation of Kinds

5. Chuck Missler, The Myths of Science, *Challenging the Myths of Astronomy in The Electric Universe,* accessed November 28, 2018, http://www.youtube.com/watch?v=CvDqrSTCcmA, 26 minutes in on the video.

6. Chuck Missler, The Myths of Science, *Challenging the Myths of Astronomy in The Electric Universe,* accessed November 28, 2018, http://www.youtube.com/watch?v=CvDqrSTCcmA.

7. Jeffrey Tomkins, PhD., *Gene Control Regions Are Protected—Negating Evolution.*

8. Mike Riddle, *The Riddle of Origins Series,* DVD series, (Answers In Genesis, Petersburg, KY 2005).

9. Richard A. Swenson, M.D., *More Than Meets The Eye,* 162.

10. Ken Ham and Britt Beemer with Todd Hillard, *Already Gone*, (Master Books, Green Forest, AZ, 2009), 81.

11. Rock Island Books, "*The Berisheet Passover Prophecy,*" accessed June 12, 2019, https://www.youtube.com/watch?v=8j5gpGTO12Y.

12. Nathaniel T. Jeanson, Bs, PhD., *Replacing Darwin*, (Master Books, Green Forest, AZ, 2009), 107

13. Dr. Stuart Firestein, *Ignorance: How it Drives Science*, (Oxford University Press, New York, NY, 2012), no page offered.

14. Ken Ham, Brett Beemer and Todd Hillard, *Already Gone*, 73.

15. Pete Briscoe with Todd Hillard, *The Surge, Six Graphs that will Change Your View of the World. . . and Life*, accessed October 10, 2012, http://getinthesurge .com/?page_id=143. 15.

16. Jerry Bergman PhD, *A select list of Science Academics, Scientists, and Scholars Who are Skeptical of Darwinism*, accessed November 28, 2018, https://www. rae.org/essay-links/darwinskeptics/

.17. Dissentfromdarwin.org, accessed, June 13, 2019, List PDF download: https:// www.discovery.org/m/2019/02/A-Scientific-Dissent-from-Darwinism-List-04092019.pdf

18. Peter Moore, "Inferential Focus Briefing," September 30, 1997

19. Facebook, "Statistics," accessed November 26, 2018, https://www.statista.com/ statistics/264810/number-of-monthly-active-facebook-users-worldwide/

20. Twitter "Statistics," accessed November 26, 2018, https://www.statista.com/sta-tistics/274564/monthly-active-twitter-users-in-the-united-states/

II: Transformers

1. Matthew 5: 45, (NAS).

2. I Corinthians 15: 51, II Timothy 3: 16, 17, Deuteronomy 31: 6, (NAS).

3. Paul Garner, *The New Creationism*, 54.

4. ". . . We are of good courage, I say, and prefer rather to be absent from the body and to be at home with the Lord." (II Cor. 5: 8), "Not everyone who says to Me, 'Lord, Lord,' will enter the kingdom of heaven, but he who does the will of My Father who is in heaven will enter.", (Matt. 7: 21), [sic].

5. James 1: 5, (NAS).

6. YouTube, "Lee Strobel Testimony," accessed November 28, 2018, https:// www.youtube.com/watch?v=E8IE9Y4wudk&t=11s.

7. YouTube, "Josh McDowell Testimony Part 1," accessed November 28, 2018, http://www.youtube.com/watch?v=d5O5nD0pyPc.

8. YouTube, "Antony Flew's conversion to theism," accessed November 28, 2018 https://www.youtube.com/watch?v=52CyiM0uiWE

9. Hebrews 3: 9, (NAS).

10. YouTube, "Ted.com talk—Conception to birth visualized—Alexander Tsiaras," accessed November 28, 2018, http://www.ted.com/talks/alexander_tsiaras_conception_to_birth_visualized.html.

12: Hope in the Passion Creator

1. YouTube, "Ted.com talk—Conception to birth visualized—Alexander Tsiaras," accessed November 28, 2018, http://www.ted.com/talks/alexander_tsiaras_conception_to_birth_visualized.html.

2. John 15: 5, (NAS).

3. I Corinthians 2: 9, (NAS).

4. Dr. Caroline Leaf, Ph.D., Communication Pathology, BSc in Logopedics and Audiology, *Switch On Your Brain*

5. James Strong, *Strong's Exhaustive Concordance of the Bible*, (Dugan Publishers, Inc., Gordonville, TN). 1. J Educ Eval Health Prof. 2008; 5: 5. Published online 2008 December 22.

Closing

1. Alistair Begg, Pastor, author. Truth For Life Bible teaching radio ministry. Video: *Sword and the Spirit Part One*, accessed August 6, 2019, https://blog.truthforlife.org/video-the-sword-of-the-spirit-part-one-by-alistair-begg.

Addendum

1. A Personal View, *ADV PHYSIOL EDUC 27:47–52, 2003* © 2003 American Physiological Society, Published online 26 July 2011 | Nature doi:10.1038/news.2011.441.

2. "Max Planck Quotes," Accessed June 15, 2019, https://www.goodreads.com/author/quotes/107032.Max_Planck

3. Federal Rules of Evidence, December 1, 2009.

4. Jeff Tollefson, "US federal agency loosens peer-review rules," Nature, July 26, 2011, doi:10.1038/news.2011.441.

References

Alaska Public Lands Information Centers, *Ice Worms*

Amplified Bible (AMP)

Armstrong, Arron Armstrong, The Gospel Project, Lifeway Christian Resources

Atkins, Dr. Peter Atkins, English chemist and a Fellow of Lincoln College at the University of Oxford

Augustine, Confessions, 1.1.1.

Batterson, Mark Batterson, Pastor, author, *Primal*

Begg, Alistair Begg, Pastor, author. Truth For Life Bible teaching radio ministry

Beemer, Britt Beemer, *Already Gone*

Bergman, Jerry Bergman PhD.

Biomimicry Research and Innovation Center (BRIC), The University of Akron

Brand, Dr. Paul Brand, *In the Likeness of God*

Briscoe, Pete Briscoe,*The Surge, Six Graphs that will Change Your View of the World. . . and Life*

Brown, Austin Brown, The Long Foundation, *Long Term Art*

Berean Study Bible, (BSB)

Burt, Daniel S. Burt, *The Biography Book*

CBS News, *Deep Sea Volcanic Vent May Offer Discoveries*

Chambers, Oswald Chambers, 20th century evangelist, author: Utmost for His Highest

Craig, Dr. William Lane Craig, an American analytic philosopher and Christian theologian. Ph.D., D. Theol.

Deem, Richard Deem, Evidence For God, *Did Albert Einstein Believe in a Personal God?*

Discovery Channel, Science, *The Human Body: Pushing the Limits*

Dissentfromdarwin.org

Dougherty, Elizabeth Dougherty, writer for MIT School of Engineering,

Encyclopedia Britanica, *Strong Force, Golden Ratio*

Ferrell, Vance Ferrell, *Marvel of God's Creation*

Firestein, Dr. Stuart Firestein, *Ignorance: How it Drives Science*

Flew, Antony Flew, SOAS, University of London; St John's College; Oxford, Signator of the Humanist Manifesto III

Forbes, *Climategate 2.0*

Fromm, Erich Fromm, *The Art of Loving*

Garner, Paul Garner, *The New Creationism*

Gelb, Michael J. Gelb, *How To Think Like Leonardo da Vinci*

Giordano, Nicholas Giordano, Professor of Political Science, Political Analyst/SR. Contributor, Suffolk Community College

Gitt, Dr. Werner Gitt, *In the beginning was information*

Graham, James R. Graham, *The Early Period*

Haakonssen , Knud Haakonssen, *The Emergence of Rational Dissent*

Ham, Ken Ham is founder and president of Answers in Genesis (USA)

Hillard, Todd Hillard, *The Surge, Six Graphs that will Change Your View of the World. . . and Life, Already Gone*

Hyman, Dr. Mark Hyman, Director of the Cleveland Clinic Center for Functional Medicine

Irwin, Terri Irwin, *20/20, Interview*

Jeanson, Nathaniel Jeanson, MS, PhD., *Replacing Darwin*

Jennings, Charles Jennings, director of neurotechnology at the MIT McGovern Institute for Brain Research

Johnson, Byron Johnson, *Religion and the Bad News Bearers*

Leaf, Dr. Caroline Leaf, PhD., Communication Pathology, BSc in Logopedics and Audiology, *Switch On Your Brain*

Lisle, Dr. Jason Lisle, *Taking back Astronomy, The Heavens Declare Creation and Science Confirms It*

Mackie, Tim Mackie, Ph.D., The Bible Project

Martin, Dr. Jobe Martin, *Incredible Creatures that Defy Evolution*

Missler, Chuck Missler, U.S. Naval Academy; UCLA, *The Myths of Science*

Moore, Peter Moore, *Inferential Focus Briefing*

National Geographic, *Brain Games*

National Malleefowl Recovery Team

New American Standard (NAS)

New International Version (NIV)

New King James Version (NKJV)

Nilson, Dr. Heribert Nilson, Professor *Synthetische Artbildung*

Piper, John Stephen Piper is an American Reformed Baptist continuationist pastor, quote

Planck, Max Planck, quote

Riddle, Mike Riddle, *The Riddle of Origins Series*

Rock Island Books, "The *Berisheet Passover Prophecy*,"

Rowling, J.K. Rowling, *Interview* at the Roald Dahl Museum in Buckinghamshire

Smith, Sam A. Smith, *Who Wrote 'the Psalms of David?*

Sproul, RC Sprul, The Holiness of God

Spurgeon, Charles Spurgeon. a nineteenth century preacher

Stark, Rodney Stark, *Religion and the Bad News Bearers*

Strobel, Lee Strobel, University of Missouri; Yale University, *The Case for a Creator*

Strong, James Strong, *Strong's Exhaustive Concordance of the Bible*

Swenson, Richard A. Swenson M.D., *More Than Meets The Eye*

The Free Dictionary, *Passion*

Tollefson, Jeff Tollefson, *US Federal Agency Loosens Peer-Review Rules*

Tomkins , Jeffrey Tomkins, Ph.D., *Gene Control Regions Are Protected—Negating Evolution*

Tsiaras, Alexander Tsiaras, *Conception to Birth; Architecture and Design of Man and Woman*

United States Government, *Federal Rules of Evidence*

Webb, R.K. Web, Knud Haakonssen, *The Emergence of Rational Dissent*

Wolfe, Hans Walter Wolff, *Anthropology of the Old Testament*

Yancey, Philip Yancey, Dr. Paul Brand, *In the Likeness of God*

Author Biography

Jim Kraft grew up in Willoughby, Ohio—a suburb of Cleveland. Jim earned his diploma from the Cleveland-based Cooper School of Art & Design and graduated with honors. He took marketing and psychology courses at Lakeland Community College. He also assisted Campus Crusade for Christ and Samaritan's Purse with promotions.

After freelancing for art studios and ad agencies, Jim began his career as an independent design and marketing consultant creating on and off-line communications for major corporations like GE Lighting, Petro Canada, American Greetings, BF Goodrich, Allstate Insurance, Carlton Cards, Honeywell, Holiday Inn, and Dutch Boy. He has also done work for regional organizations like Parkside Church, Friends Church-Willoughby Hills. His national brands include: EZPOLE Flagpoles®; SwissTech® Micro tools; BrailleWorks; and Maple Valley Sugarbush. He has also performed marketing communication services for over 80 church, Para-church and secular organizations.

Jim and his wife Tammy reside in Chardon, Ohio and have two grown children. Jim has taught marriage enrichment and biblical creation. Tammy has a degree in Family and Child Development from The University of Akron and is working as a Consultation, Training, and

Education Specialist with local school systems implementing prevention programs. She has assisted me in marriage enrichment and biblical creation classes and has been a group leader and facilitator for women's Bible studies.

The heart of it.

We can create great works that capture man's
attention and cause wonder and appreciation. We call these men
and women "Masters," and their creations—masterpieces. However,
these masterpieces do not compare with God's masterpieces. He *is*
Life's Master Designer. One of God's masterpieces is within each
of us; it is our hearts. He authored, designed and engineered our
hearts. Hearts that are capable of passion, sadness, joy, anger and,
above all else, love. Our heart is a barometer to our souls.
Unfortunately, tumultuous times can skew our perspective and
affect the condition of our hearts. The problem is, our senses can be
so deadened that we can't recognize that there is a heart/soul issue
that needs a loving touch from Heaven. Whether young or old, we
can begin to *devalue* the miracle of who we were meant to be. *Before
the Beginning...God Designed* addresses the emotional, physical
and spiritual fallout of a lost perspective, and offers the healing and
enduring hope of *God's perspective* through His *Word*, His *Son*, and
Creation. Our hearts are God's masterpieces. They are so important
to Him that He tells us to, "above all else, guard your hearts." When
we guard our hearts, knowing and owning His Word, we can more
easily grasp our Creator's heart and experience His bigness personally.
A Spirit filled heart connects us to God. If that connection renews us,
we become more like Christ. We slowly begin to understand
the incredible love and passion that God has for us.
Who else would be better to address *heart issues than* the Artist,
Author, Designer and Finisher of our hearts?